Scottyg91

JONESY

PUT YOUR HEAD DOWN AND SKATE
THE IMPROBABLE CAREER OF KEITH JONES

Keith Jones

with John Buccigross

Foreword by
Raymond Bourque

Middle Atlantic Press

www.middleatlanticpress.com

Copyright

Dedication

Brett, Malorie, and Jackson for being renewable
energy sources and letting Daddy write in peace.
Melissa for making everything, and I mean
everything, in my life possible and purposeful.
— *John Buccigross*

To my wife Laura, daughter Adrian, family,
friends and anyone I might have forgotten
who read this book thinking I would mention.
— *Keith Jones*

FOREWORD
by Ray Bourque

I played in 1,612 NHL games, won five Norris Trophies and a Stanley Cup and yet the thing I miss most about my NHL career is just being around my former teammates. Just being around the guys.

Certainly having the opportunity to play a game for a living, that I played when I was five years old, was a dream come true for me and for many of my teammates. Also, the sheer exhilaration of competition at the highest level is a rush that some of us live for. But the friends, bloopers, and practical jokes along the way are what gives the career of a professional athlete a life and a spirit that is filled with laughter, togetherness, and brotherhood that no trophy can compare with.

If there is any one lesson sports can teach children and adults it is togetherness. To stick it out in bad times, in good times and to face a challenge with a unified resolve. Does your workplace work like that? I bet not.

Another lesson sports can teach us is how much fun you can have with your "family" members.

I remember when one of my defense partners had four temporary caps on his four front teeth that had recently been knocked out. It was a big game and we were playing against the other team's big line. As usual, it was a highly competitive, pressurized situation. We were sitting on the bench getting ready to go back out on the ice when my teammate took out his mouthpiece and started talking to me. We looked down and his four caps had stuck into his mouthpiece and were just hanging on the end of it. Meanwhile, he was saying something that I couldn't even understand. I was still belly laughing as we took the ice and the puck was dropped. I'm sure the announcers said something like, "Look how calm Ray Bourque is in such a big spot."

If they only knew.

I remember when someone had put a small ball of shaving cream on top of Glen Wesley's head before he walked the entire length of Toronto's airport. You can't feel shaving cream sitting on top of your hair. Glen had fallen asleep on the plane and someone got him. The last thing you want to do is fall asleep on the team plane. You might wake up with no eyebrows.

Another favorite prank is to take someone's jeans from their locker during practice, douse them with water and throw them in a freezer at the rink. Solid as a rock.

Bob Sweeney was one of our undisputed practical joke champs. Bob would show up extra early for a team meal on game day. He would hide underneath the table, obscured by the tablecloth, and as people shuffled by getting their meals, Bob would be putting various condiments — ketchup, mayo, relish — on the tops of people's shoes.

This is the kind of stuff that you miss and laugh about and that you just don't see around a normal office. They provide a chemistry and togetherness that is vital for any organization trying to reach a difficult common goal.

Whenever you talk about the very talented hockey teams, teams that overachieve, you recognize character and chemistry. A player like Keith Jones helped create chemistry on a team because of the alternate energy source he provided. Whether it is something said in the dressing room or whether it is something done or said on the ice, that kind of energy is invaluable to a hockey team.

Now, those words or actions can be funny or serious. The most important thing is that they are well timed. In a lot of ways, Keith Jones' role was as valuable and effective as a good comedian; he had to have good timing. If you are going to do or say something for effect, it has to be well timed. Young players have a great feel of when to say something funny or silly to loosen things up and when to say or do something to get everyone together and on the same page with passion and energy. Players like Keith bring teams together. You have to have that along with talent and toughness. It is something that you can't quantify with statistics, but any player will tell you how important it is.

Keith Jones played the game hard and had a lot of fun playing it. He was the kind of player that would make you laugh in the middle of the game, even when you were in the middle of a scrum. Like when he stole Anson Carter's stick and decided to play a shift with it against us in 1999 when I was still with the Bruins. Keith was famous for having a comment that you had no comeback for. He would stump you. He had a quick, sharp mind even in the middle of a hockey game.

I miss the game for many reasons, and reading the chapters in Keith's story will help you understand why I miss it so much. Like life, there are moments as a hockey player when you laugh, cry, doubt, hope, pray, and dream. We players, like you, all have those moments, and reading Keith's story will help you understand a little bit of how the journey of an NHL player works.

The ups, the downs, and the belly laughs along the way.

Raymond Bourque

INTRODUCTION

My brother Greig died when I was fourteen years old. Nothing before or since, has had a larger impact on my life. My mom and dad, and my sisters, Barbara and Carolyn, feel the same way. That single tragedy forever changed the way I viewed the world, myself, and every obstacle I've ever faced since hearing the news that July day in 1983 in Brantford, Ontario.

My brother, Greig Jones, wasn't a great student in school, and so he made the decision to move out of the house at age fourteen for a life of labor. I was eight. Tough and as strong as an ox, Greig took a job as a stable boy, often working with the horses. The owners provided room and board, and so the farm was a place to live and work without attending school. Greig returned home when he was 20 years old and stayed with us in Brantford, a city of about 90,000 people in south-western Ontario, Canada. Inventor Alexander Graham Bell invented the telephone there on July 26th, 1874. It is also the hometown of the NHL's most prolific scorer, Wayne Gretzky.

After Greig returned home, he and I spent a lot of time together and became pretty close. He would drive me to some of my hockey games — it was always cool to have an older brother as a chauffeur. I was playing "Hub" hockey at the time, one step below the coveted AAA travel hockey league. We played games against smaller towns in and around Brantford. Most of the kids who got drafted to Major Junior played AAA travel, but kids my age were passing me by because I just wasn't growing. Since I wasn't playing travel, it put my chances of ever playing Major Junior very much in doubt.

My brother Greig was nothing like me. He was tough, worked out a lot, and really strong. He also had a quick temper and could really fight if he had to. We played ball hockey on the same team in the summer of 1983. Greig didn't have the same skill set that I had playing hockey, but he was strong and always made an effort beyond belief. If anyone came near his yappy little brother, Greig would be right there to stick up for me. That year, the summer of 1983, my brother and I became closer than we had ever been before.

As I said, Greig was an emotional person who didn't always handle adversity with as even a keel as I. One day, Greig left the house early in the morning and was gone all afternoon. When we got our local paper that afternoon, it said inside that an unidentified man was hit and killed by a train. My mom somehow knew right away it was Greig. He was dead at the age of twenty.

We still don't know if he took his own life or if he was in a state of anger and lost his concentration for a second. No one knows for sure; no one was there. But it doesn't really matter. My parents lost a son, and I lost a brother.

Greig's shocking death gave me the gift of perspective. It allowed me to take chances, speak up more, and stick up for things that I normally would not have done because of the more laid-back personality that I had.

I learned how to become aggressive and assertive when it was called for. I learned that there are times in life when you simply have to be proactive; you don't have to be a jerk about it, but you must move forward and take advantage of opportunities.

There is no doubt that the grief and pain that I both felt inside and witnessed in my parents, gave me the basis for how I deal with everything today. Watching my parents go through such pain seared an indelible mark on my consciousness. The death of a son or daughter takes years off of a parent's life. When I see something tragic happen now, I just cringe. I know how precious life is and what can happen to people when it is abruptly taken away, especially at a young age.

Age 5 in Brantford novice house league minor hockey.
I developed my smirk at a young age.

Age 6 in Brantford Novice Triple 'A' hockey.
My hairdo was a constant battle.

The season after my brother was killed, I tried out for the AAA team. One day while I was getting dressed with my friends, one of my teammates asked, "Hey, where is your brother?" Most of the guys in the room knew what had happened because Brantford was such a small town. But it had only been a month, and the news must have not gotten to this kid. I couldn't even get the words out of my mouth to tell him what happened. Someone probably took him aside afterwards to break the news.

I made the AAA team that fall. This was a small sign that, throughout my life, the things that were going to happen to me in hockey really should never have happened. It was like I was driving the car, but someone else was steering the wheel. The car wasn't moving very fast, and sometimes hardly at all, but it was always moving forward, one exit at a time. Because of what happened to my family, reverse was not an option. Forward gets you a little further from the pain.

For the rest of my hockey days, I would write down on a scrap piece of paper what level of hockey I had completed the season before. I would write down AA, AAA, Junior C, Junior B, NCAA, AHL, NHL. I would also write down, on any piece of scrap paper I could find, the names of my coaches and my statistics. I would sit and just stare at these pieces of paper. They were my homemade hockey cards, and they proved to me that every year, I was getting better and better and better. The car was moving forward. I was slowly improving. Always moving forward.

As I look back now, I see that I was slowly building something in my life. At the same time, I wasn't seriously planning on playing in the NHL. I was always realistic. I never jumped three levels of hockey like that other kid seven years older than me in our hometown. Wayne Gretzky was six years old when he played with ten year olds. When Gretzky was ten years old himself, he scored 378 goals in one season. I didn't score that many in my career. I always took one step at a time. Baby steps. Wayne was "The Great One." I was "The Late One."

Every time I needed a little strength along the way, I would look back at Greig's death, and those pieces of paper with my hockey résumé, and just say to myself, "Just suck it up. Keep going." Now, there would be times when I took my foot off the gas and was a lazy slug. I didn't do everything right all the time. I didn't run to the gym like my brother did, work out like he did, and stay in shape like he did. But I did have a mental toughness to get through times that were rocky or could have filled me with self-defeating doubt. I knew who I was, what I had to give, and what made me tick.

I never told anyone who I played with throughout my hockey career about Greig's death. Nobody knew then and nobody really knows now unless they are reading this. I didn't feel people needed to know or would feel comfortable learning that I had lost a brother. It was something that, while painful and confusing, I chose to use as a positive for me and the people who would be around me for the rest of my days. What else can we do?

I took something from my brother's death and carried it with me for life. It supplied me with a real strength, a human quality that I didn't have before. It gave me the ability to try things that didn't seem possible. I just kept pushing for it. And amazingly, I got it.

I now had the gift of knowing what was important. Professional sports are awesome, but they're fantasy. One team wins the Stanley Cup. Then everyone tries to win the next one the next year. It's an awesome thing to achieve goals like that, but I retired without winning the Stanley Cup and have not tortured myself over it. I wish I had won a Cup in order to have that passionate and everlasting bond with the guys I played with. That is real and eternal because it's based on love, respect, and honor. But I don't feel empty about my NHL career because I didn't play on a Stanley Cup winning team.

I was always a smartass and always played with a chippiness and edge even before my brother passed away. The effect my brother's tragic death had on me while growing up, and still does have to this day, is the constant reminder of just how fragile life is. I would go back to it whenever I needed it. So, I just got sent to the minors. What does that mean in the big scheme of things? It's not that big of a deal.

After Greig's death, when I would get upset, I would use my new-found vocal assertiveness. I would loudly defend myself and state my case. In my heart I would tell myself, "Get in there and do your job." I used that thinking as a foundation. I wouldn't do it every day. Maybe not even every year. I had a base built up to help me in those times without having to relive my brother's death every single time I had to deal with something. It became second nature. It became who I am.

Instead of asking, "Why is this happening?" I just went with it. If I had ever stopped and thought about what I was doing and where this hazy hockey road was leading me, I probably would have stopped and gone home because it was illogical. It would have been too much for my brain to fathom. The whole "road to the NHL" never should have been happening. But I just went with it, and it did.

I'll try, though I'm not sure I'm able, to describe adequately just how miraculous it is that I made it to the NHL and went on to make over a million dollars a year.

I just rode the wave, man. I just kept going forward without stopping and asking for directions. If I took the summer off from working out before my first NHL training camp, I never asked, "Why did I do that?" The fact that I made an NHL team after a summer of doing absolutely nothing but eating pizza and drinking beer is amazing. Absolutely amazing.

If I had any adversity-ridden angst going through my mind during my hockey career, I would draw back to how lucky I was and how unlucky my brother Greig was. The bottom line is that you live your life to the fullest and enjoy it with all your heart when things are going well. And you try your best to get through life when things are going badly.

I've always taken the time to stop and talk to anybody who wants to talk to me, whether it's around my adopted home of Philadelphia or in my travels across North America playing and now broadcasting NHL hockey. I've done this because you never know what kind of pain people might be going through. I've never shunned anyone and I never will.

This is the story of how I got to the NHL, what I did when I got there, why my career ended prematurely and painfully, and why that may have been the biggest blessing of all.

I hope you enjoy the ride.

Whatever.

Keith Jones
October 2006

CHAPTER ONE

BEER AND CHICKEN WINGS

I stopped dreaming of playing in the NHL when I was thirteen years old. I was already entrenched in reality. Nothing about my reality said "NHL player" in the slightest. You'd see a fish riding a bicycle before you would see me in the National Hockey League. I wasn't close to an elite player at thirteen, or even a fringe player on an elite team. In my mind, my remaining teenage days as a hockey player were destined to be played solely for fun and the love of the game. More precisely, for beer, girls, and chicken wings. And that was all right by me. I was having a blast playing hockey for fun. I was a guy who never lifted weights beyond twelve-ounce curls, and who never really worked out or trained in the gym. Let's get physical? No thanks.

It didn't help that Wayne Gretzky was born and raised in the same town as I. After just two years in the NHL, at age twenty, he was already one of the best players in the league, playing for the Edmonton Oilers. How could I expect to play, or even dream about playing, in the same league as he?

In 1981, Mr. Big, a chocolate bar popular in Canada, ran a promotion involving Wayne and his point total for the upcoming season. Inside the wrapper of each Mr. Big was a point total. If Wayne finished the season with the point total inside your wrapper, you would win a generic Wayne Gretzky hockey jersey with a copy of his signature across the front.

Brantford Triple 'A' Hockey. Be sure to check out head coach
Gerry Covvey's stylish plaid pants and cool shades!

At that time, Wayne was coming off his first two seasons in the NHL. His point total his rookie year was 137. He follows that up the next year with 164 points. What would he do in year three? I began to buy an obscene amount of Mr. Big chocolate bars to increase my chances of winning that jersey. And that was the beginning of my life-long love affair with any long, layered vanilla wafer, coated in caramel, peanuts and rice crisps, and covered in chocolate. Or anything close to that.

Two of the countless wrappers I accumulated through consumption have 212 for a point total. This is the area code for New York City, not an NHL season point total. No NHL player in history had ever amassed 200 points in a season. In all likelihood, I wouldn't be needing 212. But, I kept them all just in case.

I must say that was one of the greatest promotions of all time. I kept all of the wrappers, stared at them, followed Wayne game by game in the newspaper, and discarded the wrappers with point totals that Wayne had passed. It was fantasy hockey for the early '80's.

Sure enough, when the 1981-82 NHL season was all said and done, Wayne finished 92-120-212. I won not one, but two jerseys! Well, as I was getting ready for the AAA tryouts that fall, my dad hands me one of the Wayne Gretzky jerseys to wear. Talk about overestimating you son's ability! I politely declined to wear the Wayne Gretzky jersey at tryouts in an attempt to keep some of my dignity.

That year, 1983, I was 15 years old. I had skinny arms, skinny legs, no chest, and a little extra padding around the middle. Classic skinny-fat. I relied solely on whatever abilities I had at the time which didn't amount to much. I wasn't drafted into Major Junior, the highest level of amateur hockey in Canada for teenagers, mainly because I wasn't a great skater. My legs are just weren't strong enough.

I spent my early teens hoping and praying to find one measly pubic hair on my testosterone-free body. I wasn't afraid that I'd be a late bloomer, but a never bloomer. A lot of kids my age would, and did, quit in those circumstances. You had to have thick skin and keep your eyes on the prize to even have a prayer of making it. It's difficult for boys at that age, especially so in such a rough and competitive environment. Some can't take the taunts, or they missed their girlfriends or home, and they quit. Every year, more talented players than I quit and go home. I kept showing up. Somewhere. Anywhere.

I was very disappointed when I didn't get drafted into Major Junior, and nearly devastated when I was cut from a Junior B team. I had received a letter from a Junior C team but originally laughed at it as a non option. I was still thinking and dreaming of playing Major Junior. As the years rolled on, it became more and more obvious that the NHL just wasn't for me. If I couldn't get drafted into Major Junior, how in the hell could I play in the NHL?

The first two years I tried out for Junior B hockey, I got cut, so I played Junior C hockey. Junior C was two games a week and thirty games a season. A seven-year-old Mite in suburban Philadelphia plays more than thirty games a season. Here I was, entering young adulthood, playing a USA Hockey Mite schedule in Canada. In fact, if you didn't make the playoffs in Junior C, your season was over in early February. Mites played until March! How was I going to play in the NHL? But I wasn't frustrated. I was living life and having fun.

I still loved playing hockey and watching "Hockey Night In Canada" without any thoughts at all that I would actually play in the NHL. I dreamt of playing in Maple Leaf Gardens as a kid until, like I said, about thirteen. Professional hockey had always interested me, but as I hit my teenage years, I just didn't think it was for me. It wasn't so much that I didn't think I was good enough, although there were probably plenty of people who would have said that. To me, it was more like, "it isn't for me."

I tried out for Junior B as a sixteen-year-old, and got cut. Deservedly. I could have possibly played as a fourth line guy, but I wasn't really ready physically. The Junior B team I tried out for was my hometown team, the Brantford Classics. Rob Blake was on that team. After getting cut, I had to turn to that Junior C letter from a team in Paris, Ontario (population 7,000) that I originally scoffed at playing for.

But, I wasn't even guaranteed to make the Paris Mounties because in Junior C hockey, each team is allowed only five "imports." If you didn't live within a certain radius of the town where the team played, you were deemed an import. I tried out and was one of the last guys, maybe the last, to make the Mounties. I was relieved to have somewhere to play, because had I not made it, I would have, without question, quit playing hockey. Despite being about as low as one could be, I had a great time playing Junior C. For the first time the equipment and the sticks were free! And, Paris is about a fifteen-minute drive from Brantford, so it was close and convenient.

I began my Junior C career as a second/third-line-type player and had a blast doing it. As I said, we played just thirty games in the season. So, we had plenty of time between games and our one practice a week to be normal teenagers.

The atmosphere was perfectly suited for my personality. We played in little towns and sometimes got as many as 1,000 fans in an intimate arena. I thoroughly enjoyed playing in this non-pressurized environment. I played solely for the love of the game, never thinking NHL even once. Furthermore, because I knew the coach, Jerry Convey, I was de facto "part time G.M." of the team, and helping him decide which farm boys to keep and which to cut was a lot of fun.

Our routine was simple. We practiced once a week, played twice a week, and went out to eat chicken wings and drink beer in between. I like it so much, and drank so many beers, that I didn't want to have to drive back home to Brantford after practices and games. So, I moved in with a family in Paris towards the end of my first Junior C season. My parents paid fifty bucks a week for me to stay with the family of my teammate Keith Roswell. Keith was an average player, but a good guy, so I used my "Assistant G.M." status to keep him on the team.

It is always great to learn from one of the best- here I am with Bobby Orr.

The Roswell house was so different from what I was used to back in Brantford. The Roswells were great to me, and I really appreciated the way they opened their home to me. They were hard working people who didn't really have a lot. I, meanwhile, had a nice middle-class upbringing. My dad was the Superintendent of Special Education and my mom was a housewife who kept everything in order. My dad was born in Wales and came to Canada at age seventeen. He tells me he had trouble in school as a kid and claims he was voted "least likely to succeed." The fact that he became superintendent was a good sign to me in terms of achieving unlikely or unpredictable things.

Anyway, my billet home in Paris was an absolute mess. A big difference from my orderly home. At the Roswell home, we ate dinner and then, for a week, the dishes would sit there on the counter and pile up in the sink. The mashed potatoes coagulated with the corn on the cob, forming a substance that was probably toxic.

My bed in Paris was in the middle of the dining room, and the Roswell family had a dog who shit all over the house. When I got up at night to go to the bathroom, I had to bring a flashlight with me in order to avoid the many turds strewn across the house. Despite the doggy wallop slalom course I had to navigate on a nightly basis, I stayed with the Roswell family for two years.

My first year of Junior C went pretty well. I didn't step in too much crap at the Roswell's house and I scored 26 goals and had 13 assists in 30 games. We missed the playoffs, though, and so I headed home to Brantford in early February. Short and sweet.

During the summer of 1986, I finally began to really grow. I actually had been slowly growing during the previous season in Paris. Throughout that season, and counting the summer, I grew almost six inches.

It's hilarious how small I am in the first team picture in Paris. I was a little, tiny guy. I made Darren Pang look like Zdeno Chara. Even though I was growing, I still haven't gained any weight. I was seventeen years old and 160 pounds. I still never worked out, lifted weights, or ran. During the summer, I went out with friends, drank beers, and just fooled around town. It was a great time to be a kid.

That fall, the Brantford Junior B team was suspended for the upcoming year because of a huge bench-clearing brawl they had the previous season.

I was actually at the game that got the Brantford Classics suspended for a year. It was the most unbelievable display of violence that I've ever seen. The two teams just beat the hell out of each other. Eight of the guys on the opposing St. Catharine's team were so frightened by the mayhem that they ran into the dressing room while the other teammates were left to fend for themselves. Two Brantford guys held a St. Catharine's guy's arms while another Brantford player punched him in the head. There were dropkicks with skates on. It was surreal. Definite *Slap Shot* DVD extra material.

Because of the yearlong team suspension, there was no Junior B team in Brantford to try out for in the fall of 1986. I was sure I had developed enough since the last time I was cut from the team, to make it the next time around. But again, because of the suspension, I had no local team to go out for. I would have to go somewhere else if I wanted to try out for Junior B. Rob Blake also had to find another team as a result of the suspension and ended up playing for the Stratford Cullitons.

I decided to go to Cambridge, Ontario, where I was actually born, and try out for the Junior B team there. I lasted one day. I could have made it, but out of the blue, I just said "Ahhh, I'm going to go and play Junior C again." I just wasn't in the mood that day. It didn't feel right and so I left. Someone was steering my car.

I drove back to Paris and told the Mounties I was going to play with them again. It was a smart move. I continued to love playing. We rode a yellow school bus to the games. Girlfriends were allowed on the bus. We wore sweatpants, hats, and cowboy boots to the games we played in all those small Canadian towns. And yes, we had bench-clearing brawls. Though still a little guy, I was usually the one to start the melees. Luckily, I had guys willing to protect me. By the end of the brawls, everyone would be wondering where I was and I'd be under the bench going "Is it over yet?"

There was a bench-clearing brawl against a team from the little town of New Hamburg. A real haymaker-fest. At the end of the night there were five New Hamburg guys and five of our guys in the same hospital room. Their beds were all lined up together like players on a bench. I went to visit my teammates the night of the game and I found our opponents in the same room. Everyone was laughing and joking around just hours after pummeling each other. Only in hockey.

Those were interesting times to be playing Junior C. The passion at the lower levels of hockey is amazing and it was a great experience. It was scary at times, but as exciting and organic as hockey gets.

My second year playing for the Paris Mounties, the 1986-87 season, I turned eighteen and finished with 39 goals and 38 assists. My penalty minutes went from 61 to 136 since my growth spurt made it easier to mix it up on the ice with more confidence and frequency. We didn't make the playoffs for the second straight year, so my season ended again in early February.

As I had the year before, I made ten dollars a week in gas money playing Junior C hockey. Ten bucks! I went in during the second season and successfully negotiated for ten extra dollars of gas money if we made the playoffs. Twenty bucks a week. Since I was living in Paris anyway and not commuting home, I really thought I got them good. It wouldn't be the first time I use my negotiating skills to profitable use. However, since we didn't make the playoffs I never enjoyed the raise in gas money.

In early 1987, as my second season with Paris was winding down, and high school graduation loomed in the near future, someone on the team brought in a media guide from a college hockey team. I had never really thought about going to college. I was an average student. My motto was "C's get degrees" and I lived by it. Therefore, I never really thought of college hockey. I never read any books and didn't develop any study habits, which is unusual because my Dad has his Masters in English and is obviously a big believer in school, what with being a superintendent. But I never had the patience, or enjoyed the classroom enough, to think about college.

So, I saw this media guide that the teammate brought in from the University of Massachusetts at Lowell. As I scanned down the roster, I saw some of the names are of guys who had played Junior B hockey. Like I said, I had never thought about college because I didn't see myself as a student or as good enough to play at that level. But, as I looked at that college hockey media guide, out of the blue, a light went on in my head.

With a couple of weeks left in the season, I took the G.M. of our Junior C team, Bob Rayfield, aside and said to him, "Bob, this is what I'm going to do. I'm going to go play Junior B next year. Then I'm going to get drafted into the NHL, go to college, and then I'm going to go play in the NHL. That's what I'm going to do."

Just like that. Out of nowhere, in the halls of a dark, cold hockey arena, at the tail end of a Junior C season, I set an unlikely course for my life. The thought of playing in the NHL had never seriously entered my mind until I looked into that media guide and saw opportunity. At least that's what I thought I saw. It didn't really make any sense. There wasn't any logic to support my plan.

I said it and I believed it when I said it. I wouldn't go on to work hard to get it, but I said it, leave it at that, and walk away. I didn't go home that summer with "Eye of the Tiger" or some other Rocky-movie music ringing in my ears. I didn't get all fired up and crank out 1,000 push-ups a day. I announced my plan that one day. And when I said it, I felt like it felt right. It sounded right. It didn't sound silly or outlandish. But again, I didn't change a thing in terms of working out or preparing physically for this arduous task. I figured I'd just have fun with my friends, not work out very much, and play hockey when I felt like playing hockey. It was a bit of a contradiction, I know, but I was pretty consistent in my inconsistency.

The following season grew closer and I was obviously physically ready for Junior B. It's just a question of where I would play. The Brantford Classics were up and running again after serving their yearlong suspension. But I still had a bad taste in my mouth with Brantford. I never made their team out of Midget hockey when I tried out the first time, so I really didn't think I wanted to play for them.

Meanwhile, another friend of mine from back in Brantford, Kenny Wilson, had just sat out a year of hockey. Kenny went to Niagara Falls where the owners have a reputation for really taking care of their players. Kenny played there and had a great time. He is a year older than me and I always kind of looked up to him. So, anything he said to me I took with a certain amount of respect. Kenny said to me, "Hey, Larry, why don't you come up and try out for the Junior B team in Niagara Falls?" He called me Larry because my middle initial is L and his nickname for me was "Larry the Loser."

I said, "OK. I'll try out for Niagara Falls."

Niagara Falls had already sent someone down during my previous Junior C season in Paris to watch me play. Since they showed a little interest in me, that was enough for me to go try out for them.

I went to their training camp and tried out with no guarantee I would make the team. I showed up at training camp with a really old, broken-down pair of skates. The first day of training camp I was falling down all over the ice like a drunken sailor. I felt just terrible about my performance and thought I was toast. I called my dad and told him that I had to get a new pair of skates if I was to have any shot of making the Niagara Falls Canucks. Dad said OK.

We went to a sporting goods store in Niagara Falls, called Cupolos, and got a new pair of skates. They fit really well and were really solid on my feet. The guys at the store did a really good job of fitting the skates for me. I had never really paid attention before to fitting and how important it is for your skates to fit for you to play at your highest level.

I got the new skates, and after a couple of days of breaking them in, I started feeling really good on them. Although I didn't light it up by any means, I played well enough in an exhibition game to make the team as a fourth line player. To celebrate, my dad came back up to visit and we went to dinner at a Big Boy restaurant in Niagara Falls.

As we waited for our food to arrive I said, "Dad, I want to tell you something. I'm so happy I did this. I'm so happy I made Junior B. This is so great. One day, I can tell my kids that I played Junior B hockey."

CHAPTER TWO
B THE BALL

All of a sudden, things started to happen for me playing Junior B hockey for the Niagara Falls Canucks. Junior B is two steps below Major Junior, but you could still play college if you played Junior B. There is Major Junior, Tier 2 Junior A, and then Junior B.

Now, in Junior B, for every Gilbert Dionne, there seemed to be a character or an episode right out of the movie "Slap Shot." We had a few at Niagara Falls, but the story I'm about to tell you was one of the best.

So, there we were, early on in training camp during tryouts, when this big 6´5˝ guy named Mike Petkovich comes out on the ice. Well, you can't help but notice this guy because A) he is huge, and B) he can't skate. I mean he can't skate at all. I'm looking around thinking, "What is this dude's story? He can't even get around the ice." So, I ask my friend Kenny Wilson and Kenny tells me that Mike has been a goalie his whole life and the Masterson brothers, who run our team, brought him in to "add some muscle to the squad in case we ever needed it." Mike was sent to some summer camps in an attempt to work on his skating, but it did not appear to help. Once the regular season starts, we don't see Mike anymore.

Well, during a game in November, one of the goons on the Welland Cougars named Tim Herbert — and he looks every bit like a Herbert — takes a shot at one of our top players, Mike Dunham. Dunham is injured and is expected to miss about six weeks. Well, the next day at practice, off the farm and on the ice stumbles Mike Petkovich. We help Mike around the ice a few times and he is deemed ready for our next game, which happens to be against Welland. Meanwhile,

Mike's parents are in Mexico finishing up a vacation, oblivious to what's about to take place with their son.

Before the game with Welland, in the pre-game skate, we literally help Mike around the ice like he had just torn both his ACLs and had a crushed pelvis. He is laughing and understands the absurdity of it all. Mike's a good guy with a good sense of humor.

The game against Welland begins and Mike stays on the bench for the entire game. Finally, in the third period, he gets the tap on the shoulder from our coach, "You're up!" The players are lining up as Mike meanders across the way toward the face-off, which is in front of the Welland bench. I'm surprised he's on the ice now because Herbert, Welland's goon, isn't even out there. This doesn't matter to Mike.

He spots Herbert sitting on the bench, wobbles over, takes his stick over his head, brings the blade back to his heels, comes over the top, and tomahawks Herbert right across the head. He breaks his full shield, I-Tech visor in half, and cracks Herbert's helmet right down the middle. The entire Welland team jumps Mike and a brawl ensues. Sticks and punches are flying. Welland's coach Mike Healy loses some blood trying to break up the mayhem.

Obviously the Mastersons and our stick-wielding ex-goalie are punished. Petkovich is given two match penalties, is arrested at 3 a.m., and charged by Niagara Regional Police with assault with a weapon. Herbert is treated and released at a local hospital with a slight concussion.

I go to a hearing on the matter and the Commissioner asks me, "Is it not true that the player in question was a goaltender his whole life?" I reply, "Yeah, but they sent him to some hockey schools and he really started to improve. He's done a lot of good things for us in practice!" Meanwhile, he hasn't been to a practice all year since the first tryout. It is all one of the most surreal things I've ever experienced. And so for Tim Herbert, he tells the local newspaper, the *Niagara Falls Review*, that he is retiring from hockey, saying, "I've had enough." I bet!

It was all one of the most surreal things I'd ever experienced. A couple of years later at college I was watching CNN in one of the cafeterias at college. The fact that I was watching CNN is amazing in and of itself. Anyway, I was bored and eating lunch and I looked over at the television and it said: TWO MEN OVER NIAGARA FALLS IN A BARREL. Well, that got my attention since I just played in Niagara Falls. This is big time TV in 1989. All of the media were there, and the police are waiting to fish this barrel out of the water and arrest whoever is inside. It's decent drama to watch unfold.

Well, who comes out of the barrel but some guy named Peter Debernardi and Clyde Petkovich, the brother of our ex-goalie, stick-wielding, enforcer for a game, Mike Petkovich! I couldn't believe what I was seeing. These two just made history as the *first team to go over Niagara Falls together in a barrel*. Clyde comes out of the barrel completely naked except for a CCM hockey helmet, necktie, cowboy boots and a beer. CNN superimposes a leaf over his privates, which makes it even funnier. Well, Clyde steps up to the microphone and says seriously and emphatically, "I did this so kids will stay off drugs!"

Since no one was around with me watching all of this, I wondered if it was really happening. I used to spend some time at the Petkovich house because another brother, Todd Petkovich, played at St. Lawrence University and had a cup of coffee in the AHL with the St. Catharines, and then Newmarket, Saints. I knew this naked guy who just crawled out of a barrel! But, I still wasn't sure it really just happened. "This must be a dream," I remember thinking.

Years later I Googled "Clyde Petkovich" and sure enough there was the whole Niagara Falls barrel story. I guess it really did happen. The thing is, Clyde wasn't even planning on jumping the falls that day until he met some guy at a local bar who was bummed out that his partner had just backed out of making possible history. Listening to this depressed guy while enjoying an ice cold beverage, Clyde tells the guy, "I'll do it with you!" And the rest is history.

The 1987-88 season started in Niagara Falls, and like dominos, things began to fall my way. One of my teammates, Mike Zaruta, left the team. He got homesick, like a lot of kids get playing Junior hockey across Canada, and he went back home to Chatham, Ontario. As a result of this sudden vacancy, I got a chance to skate on the top line.

By then my skates were really broken in. I was comfortable with my new team and my new league, and the timing was just perfect to take advantage of the opportunity.

The first game of the 1987-88 season, I went out and scored 5 points. You are never quite sure you belong when you go from one level of hockey to the next. I felt like I belonged in Junior B after that night. From there, I went on to have multiple 5-, 6-, and even 7-point games playing for Niagara Falls.

Gilbert Dionne, Marcel's REALLY younger brother (by nineteen years) was on our team at that time as a seventeen year old. It was his second year of Junior B hockey. He went on to play Major Junior with the Kitchener Rangers for two seasons, and then 223 NHL games. He was on Montreal's 1993 Stanley Cup winning team.

The '87-88 season was rolling along, and things were going well for me and the Canucks. I always played with an aggressive edge to my game – without the fighting part. I just wasn't big enough or strong enough for fisticuffs. I was getting stronger on my skates in some areas on the ice, like in the corners, but I still wasn't as strong a skater that I should have been at this point in my hockey career. I was still falling down a lot and landing on my knees all the time.

That November my coach, Terry Masterson, called me into his office. Terry was the coach, and his twin brother Tim Masterson was the G.M. of the Niagara Falls Canucks. Their dad bought the team in 1972 and the boys ran the team and still do. They love to win and really take care of the guys on the team.

My coach Terry tells me that the Director of Player Personnel & Recruitment from the Washington Capitals, Jack Button, wants to talk to me. One of Button's scouts, Sam McMaster, told Button he liked something he saw in me. I found out later that McMaster was at one of our games to scout a younger player for St. Catharines.

It turns out, while McMaster was checking out the young kid, he noticed me. He sees something in me that I never saw in myself. His report says I am a smart and intense playmaker who has some size and goes to the net without fear. No one on the Niagara Falls team was even rated on any draft lists yet, so Jack Button was surprised when McMaster told him that I was the best player on the ice that night.

My first reaction to Terry Masterson about the Capitals being interested was incredulity.

"Come on!" I say, with my nose turned up. "What are you talking about?"

I'm just a fan of the game. Playing some hockey and not worrying about the next minute, much less the next day, much less a couple of years. Much less the freaking NHL.

"What do you mean, the Washington Capitals?" I say.

Terry Masterson says he is serious and that the Capitals are wondering if I'm interested in going to college the following year. At the same time, Terry and the Niagara Falls Canucks also have an interest in keeping me since I have one more year of Junior eligibility as a nineteen year old. They aren't really pushing this college thing since I would really tear up the league if I come back for another season. They ask me what I think, and I'm like, "Go to college? I don't know."

I had been out of school for a year. Mostly to appease my parents, I signed up for grade 13 at Niagara Falls High School, where I thought I'd get some added credits and pretend to try to get into college. I had already been turned down because my grades weren't high enough. However, after all of that, I ended up not going to grade 13 to get those added credits.

Meanwhile, I was making a little money on the side moving furniture for my girlfriend's family back in Cambridge, Ontario. They were just getting into the moving company business and my future looked to be in that back-breaking line of work. The family was talking about sending me off to moving company school to learn the ropes of the business. I assume they wanted me to be able to support their daughter in case we ever got married and I needed a job.

The work was awful. I'm a grunt making seven dollars an hour, driving around with these guys with cigars hanging out of the side of their mouths. To make matters worse, I'm weak! I have to carry all these heavy refrigerators and stuff from house to truck and truck to house. It was terrible. You have to empty a house out, move the stuff, and then fill the new house back up again. It's hell. I feel for these guys who make this their life's work.

After contemplating my immediate future, I say to Terry and Tim Masterson about this college thing, "I don't know, I think I'd just rather stay here."

They liked that answer.

In the meantime, I didn't tell anyone about the Capitals' interest, because I didn't really believe it and I didn't want to embarrass myself if it all came to nothing.

The '87-88 season continued in Niagara Falls. The team was winning and I was playing really well. Our record for the season ended up 35-5-2, and we won the Golden Horseshoe Junior B League. About two weeks after my coach first told me of the Capitals interest, I find out the Washington Capitals want to talk with me one-on-one.

Washington says they are definitely interested in me. Scouts like Mike Abbamont, and Hugh Rogers tell me I'm not ready by any means to even come to camp or anything at the moment. But with some seasoning maybe I can turn into something. They think college would be a good place for me to develop as a hockey player. So, Jack Button of the Capitals says, "Would you be interested in going to college?"

I said, "I don't think so."

The Capitals, like any NHL team, are used to kids jumping at any opportunity to move their games forward. But, I'm obviously not your average bird. The Capitals are a bit stunned at my response.

Button says, "Let me get this straight. Are you telling me you don't want to go to college to see if you might be able to play in the NHL one day? What are you talking about?"

I say, "Well, what do you mean? What is it really? Where are these schools?"

I was kind of like the Unfrozen-Caveman/Lawyer character Phil Hartman played on *Saturday Night Live*: "Ladies and gentlemen of the jury, I'm just a caveman. I fell on some ice and later got thawed out by some of your scientists. Your world frightens and confuses me!" I mean, I had a girlfriend, a job, and I just didn't want to leave home. I knew I had that plan to go to college and then the NHL, but there was no rush. I was comfortable doing what I was doing. And there are hundreds, maybe thousands of kids who feel the same way I did. They are in love and don't want to leave their hometown or whatever to take the long, hard road to the NHL. Most of them are simple, small-town kids who don't push themselves just that little more to see how far they can go. There were a lot of better players than me who just never pushed on because of some of the reasons I just stated: love, homesickness, fear of the unknown, parental pressure, or comfort with the life they are living. I always recognized all of those better players during my years growing up and it always kept me grounded throughout my career.

So, the Capitals plead with me to just meet with some colleges and I finally agree. Michigan State, Miami of Ohio, and Western Michigan are the schools the Capitals first contact. NHL teams like for colleges to keep this process hush-hush so other NHL teams don't get wind of an obscure prospect. If one of the schools offers a full scholarship, then the team will more than likely draft the player at the following draft, unless they are completely overmatched. College hockey is free development for NHL teams, and the colleges gain access to players they perhaps wouldn't find through normal recruiting procedures. Word spreads quickly about late-in-the-game players like me.

The schools are talking to me in November and December. Letters of intent are usually signed in October. By then, colleges are all done with recruiting, have already committed their allotment of scholarships, or have no more players to look at. Colleges wouldn't have any information on me because I played Junior C the year before. All they really have on me is the little Junior B I am currently playing.

The Capitals go around and sell me to colleges who have a spot or two open on their roster. The colleges look to NHL teams like Washington to provide an overlooked Junior B player that can help them without affecting the school's recruiting budget. It is a good deal for everybody. The school, the NHL team, and for the player, in this case, me.

UMass Lowell, Northeastern, and Western Michigan are the three schools that show a little interest in me after Miami of Ohio and Michigan State drop out. The assistant coaches are coming to some of my games and the routine is the same: I meet the coaches and they say they want me to come on a recruiting trip.

I'm thinking, this is awesome! I'm still not sold on leaving home and need to be pushed a little bit in one direction or the other. Then again, the schools are not sold on me either. But I'm still excited at the attention and the choices now in front of me that don't include loading and unloading moving vans.

After my initial hesitation, my mind was catching up to the unexpected process, and settling in to the possibilities. When you rehearse your life in your mind or on a piece of paper, you are able to handle things more clearly when you think it through a bit.

Meanwhile, an older friend from Brantford, Paul Polillo, was playing at Western Michigan at the time. He was a big star there – a small centerman and a real talented player who was among the leaders in the CCHA in scoring. He was drafted by the Pittsburgh Penguins in the 1988 Supplemental Draft. But Paul was one of those players who didn't really want to leave home. He was way better than me but didn't have that hunger and drive to block out the world and go for it.

Anyway, since I know Paul, and Western Michigan is only a five-hour drive from Brantford, I visit there first. I figure I can go to college at Western and keep the girlfriend back home. This is a plus. I take my tour of the Western Michigan campus. The guys on the team take me out and show me a good time with some pizza and beers. I have a good visit and think the campus is really nice. By the end of the weekend, the head coach, Bill Wilkinson, says he wants to see me in his office. I figure he's going to say he really wants me to join his team in the fall and would I sign a letter of intent to attend Western Michigan right here, right now. But, he doesn't say any of this.

When I get into Wilkinson's office, he doesn't offer me anything. He says with a kind of a confused tone in his voice, "I don't know what we got here with you. I like some things you do, but I can't get a feel for how you play or your game. I got to think about what I want to do with you. I need to watch you more."

I was hoping Bill Wilkinson would ask me right there to come to Western Michigan. It was close to home and convenient to get back and forth to my buddies and my girlfriend. My initial hesitation was turning into tunnel vision. Western Michigan feels right.

By then, I didn't want to fly to Boston later in that week to visit Northeastern and UMass Lowell, who got in the game after the word spread in the small world of college hockey as it often does. Flying is a pain to me and I wanted the school I chose to be close to home anyway.

I wanted the best of both worlds.

Wilkinson comes back to see me play again at Niagara Falls a few days before I'm set to fly to Boston to visit Lowell and Northeastern. Usually when the head coach comes to see you, you know a school is looking to make a final decision since the assistants do a lot of the preliminary scouting and interviews. I'm in the beginning of a very good year. I play 40 games in 1987–88, score 50 goals, and get 80 assists for 130 points in the 40 games.

Coach Wilkinson doesn't not say anything after the Sunday game. I'm supposed to leave for Boston the following Thursday to visit Lowell and Northeastern. It's late in the game now, and Wilkinson's indecisiveness is not making me feel too good about my chances at Western Michigan.

So, it's Thursday morning and I'm packing for my trip to Boston. It looks now that my decision will come down to these two schools. It's far from home, too far, but if this is where I have to go to continue with my plan, then I guess I'll have to do it.

I'm about to leave for the airport when the phone rings. It's Bill Wilkinson. I won't be flying to Boston today. Wilkinson says, "I was thinking about you and your game. I think that I'd like to offer you a full scholarship."

I say, "Great, I'll take it."

CHAPTER 3

"DRAFTED? WHAT DO YOU MEAN, DRAFTED?"

I had one more summer before I headed to Kalamazoo, Michigan to begin my college hockey career at Western Michigan. I'd met with the Washington Capitals a few times, but still didn't really believe the brief discussion would amount to anything in the end, even though I took their recommendation to go to college. The first time I was told the Capitals had an interest in me I didn't believe it at all. Once I realize the contact with the Caps was real, I was still skeptical that anything would come of it.

Jack Button was one of the guys talking to me. Jack Button, who passed away in 1996, was the Capitals' Director of Player Personnel and Recruitment at the time. The fact that the Capitals showed any interest kind of had some personal coincidence for me. You see, the first NHL game I ever attended as a kid was in Maple Leaf Gardens. My neighbor, Paul Baker, and his parents had four tickets and they asked me to go to the game with them. Our seats were right behind the bench for a Maple Leaf-Washington Capitals game. Yep, the Capitals.

The tickets actually belonged to his parents. They sat higher up in Maple Leaf Gardens to start the game and gave us the seats right behind the Toronto bench. For the first period we sat on the ice, then we switched seats with his parents so we both could get a close up look at the sights and sounds of the National Hockey League.

The thing that blows me away watching my first NHL game, considering my ideal seat, is not the speed, or the skating, or the strength of the NHL player. What blows me away is the language! I'd never heard such swearing in my life. It was like a sailor's convention. We didn't have any cable TV yet, so for a kid in the late 70s this was Vocabulary 101. You haven't lived until you hear Borje Salming drop multiple F-bombs with a Swedish accent.

These guys were just animals and they STUNK! I mean they smelled like a three-month-old catfish lying on the hood of a Buick. In July. In downtown Phoenix. The entire spectacle just bombarded my teenage senses. It smelled like teen spirit. It was nirvana.

At the end of the first period we switch seats with my friend's parents. Well, after watching the second period away from all the real action, my friend and I can't wait to watch the third period back down near the ice. However, after my bud's parents got a load of the scene during the second period near the Maple Leaf bench — the stench, the swearing, and the savagery — they were like, "No, way are you sitting back down here again! Get back up top, kids!" They were horrified at the language. Or maybe they liked it.

I'm not really sure which.

Fast-forward ten years, and it's NHL draft day 1988 at the hallowed Montreal Forum. This is the Mike Modano, Jeremy Roenick, Rod Brind'Amour, Teemu Selanne, Mark Recchi, Rob Blake, and Link Gaetz draft.

Now, I have no idea it is NHL draft day on this June day in 1988. There is no World Wide Web yet to follow every move of western civilization. Plus, I have one year of Junior B under my belt. People like me don't get drafted. They apply for summer work with the town recreation department.

I'm not staying up counting the hours down to the 1988 NHL draft. I'm not on any draft boards. Besides, I know I'm heading to Western Michigan to play NCAA hockey in a couple of months, so the draft isn't an urgent matter. Plus, I hadn't heard from the Capitals after their contact during my Junior B season in Niagara Falls. I assume I'm just one of hundreds of guys they talked to and there are only twelve rounds in the draft. I'm out of their minds by now. They would have called me at least once if they thought there was a chance of drafting me, wouldn't they? By this time I'm really happy I never told anyone about the shiny business card the Capitals handed me the season before.

Because I'm thinking now, "This ain't happening."

On NHL draft day 1988, I take my girlfriend to Flamboro Downs in Brantford for a summer afternoon of harness racing. Not actual riding, but to watch harness racing. I know how to woo the women. Now, my girlfriend's dad is a season-ticket holder at Maple Leaf Gardens and also a member of the Hotstove Lounge, which was a restaurant within the arena. Whenever I was home from hockey season, we would head up to Toronto, about an hour from Brantford. He really took care of me when we went to those games. I was nineteen, so I could drink beer at the time, there was food waiting in between periods, and I was sitting in the stands watching the games as an absolute fan. That's it. Just a fan.

I wasn't a hockey prospect, or even a dreamer imagining myself out there on Maple Leaf Gardens ice. I was just a fan with no idea that I might even speak to a scout from an NHL team. I mean, there were kids my age playing in those NHL games! So, I just sat and watched.

It never entered my mind that I could possibly be out there on NHL ice one day. I mean, I wasn't in the same universe as those guys.

Therefore, there was no pressure because I was completely ignorant of how everything kind of works and the different paths all these NHL players take. I'm amazed now what my mindset was like then. But, it served me well.

Now, if you'll bear with me for a moment, I should mention that my girlfriend had dated a Junior A hockey player from St. George, Ontario named Don Pancoe. As you can imagine, this can cause some issues when you are young and having a hard time getting out of Junior C. Now, my girlfriend's parents always seemed to like Donny more than me because he played Major Junior. Maybe they felt they had a better chance at a son-in-law in the NHL. Not that it mattered. They are now multimillionaires with that moving company I worked for, Mcarthur Express.

Anyway, earlier that summer, my girlfriend's dad, Walter Scott, asks me if I can drive a truck with an emergency shipment to Montreal, six-and-a-half hours away. I say sure. On my way to Montreal I need gas. I pull into a gas station and the attendant asks me what kind of gas I need. I say regular, although I'm not sure. I figure the odds are with me. Before I continue with the road trip, I stop and pick up my cousin Allan to keep me company for the long ride. I ask him what kind of gas he thinks the truck takes since I wasn't sure I put the right gas in. He really doesn't know either. Mind you, this isn't Bill Gates and Paul Allen having this discussion in a moving truck.

I pull into another gas station and ask the attendant what kind of gas he thinks it takes. He says, "Diesel." So, I say fill it up with Diesel. We now have two different gasolines working in the truck. I'm suddenly concocting the world's most flammable mixed drink.

All of the sudden rockets start shooting out of the tailpipe. Big loud noises. Come to find out, I was correct the first time when I put the regular gasoline in. I call my girlfriend and tell her I think I messed up the truck with the incorrect gasoline. She says to try and find a place to look at it. So, I pull up to this service station with three guys sitting in front who have about seven teeth between them. It was like the front row of a Willie Nelson concert. This one guy looks up and says to me, "Ralph! Why did you leave the wedding reception so early?"

Ralph? I immediately play along, "Oh, I got tired."

The hillbilly responds, "It was your sister's wedding, Ralph!"

So, I tell these guys, who think I'm some dude named Ralph, about my problem.

41

And the one guy says, "I was about to leave, but anything for you Ralph."

So, the dude gets a garden hose and starts to siphon out the gas with his mouth. He gets it going, spits out the gas, and eventually gets all of the gas out of the truck. We fill the tank back up with the correct gasoline and I offer him an extra twenty bucks for drinking some of my diesel.

He says, "Ralph, I can't take your money. You know that." I have a half hour conversation with a guy who thinks I am someone else. Named Ralph.

A few days later Walter Scott, the boss, gets the receipts, sees what I had done with the dueling gasolines, and buries me at the Sunday dinner table in front of everybody. Mr. Scott must have been thinking, "What is my daughter doing with this doorknob?"

Well, 1988 was the ex-boyfriend's draft year as well and all I heard that spring was my girlfriend's parents saying, "Oh, I wonder what round Donny is going to get drafted?" That's all I hear. Donny this. Donny that.

Now, I still haven't told anybody about the couple of conversations I have had with the Washington Capitals out of fear that nothing would come of it and I would look like a desperate weasel making something up like that.

So, my girlfriend and I return from a stimulating afternoon of harness racing. We arrive at my house, get out of the car and walk toward the house where my dad is standing with a weird kind of look on his face. My dad doesn't usually show much emotion, so this look has me a little concerned.

I say, "What's wrong?"

He replies, "You've been drafted."

I say, "What do you mean, drafted? We're going to war?"

And my dad says, "No! You've been drafted in the NHL!"

I say, "What? What are you talking about?"

My dad tells me that Bryan Murray, coach of the Washington Capitals, called my Mom and asked for me. She said I wasn't there and so he asked her if he could ask a question about me. She said sure. Murray asks, "How old is your son?"

Mom says, "He's nineteen."

"When was he born?"

"November 8, 1968," says Mom.

So, the Capitals hold the phone so my Mom can hear the announcement during the seventh round of the NHL draft.

"With the 141st selection of the 1988 NHL draft, the Washington Capitals select Keith Jones, Niagara Falls Junior B Canucks." (141 is also how many career assists I would retire with in the NHL.)

But wait. The NHL calls a timeout after the Capitals announce my name. That's right, the draft is halted. The NHL comes over to the Capitals table because they have no idea who I am. I'm not on any lists of eligible players to be drafted. The NHL has no idea who the hell I am. After confirming my existence, age, and eligibility, the NHL OK's the selection and I'm drafted by the Washington Capitals.

My mom is excited. When I get inside the house she says I have to be home at eight o'clock because the Capitals are going to call. Bryan Murray does indeed call to congratulate me and tell me to go off to college and we'll see what happens in the future. Then he says one of their scouts really wants to talk to me and it's Sam McMaster, now a scout with the Columbus Blue Jackets.

Sam says, "Keith, I'm your godfather. I told those guys we got to take you. They wanted someone else and I told them we're taking you! You're going to make it to the NHL. I know you're going to play." Needless to say, when I got off the phone I was really excited. No one had EVER said anything like that to me before.

The best part of the story is that the old boyfriend, Don Pancoe, who had played Major Junior with Shayne Corson, Keith Gretzky, and Keith Primeau, did indeed get drafted. But, not until the TENTH round. Fifty-two picks after me by the Pittsburgh Penguins. (He would never make it to the NHL.)

So, my girlfriend's parents saw the news that two area kids got drafted into the NHL. Keith Jones in the seventh round and Don Pancoe in the tenth round! They couldn't believe it. When I got to my girlfriend's house after the "news" broke, I got the impression they were disappointed that I went before their beloved Don Pancoe! I was like, "What the heck did I do?"

Later that weekend we went out on my girlfriend's dad's boat and he was still in shock over me getting drafted. It was a nice summer day on the boat and I took off my shirt to get some sun. My girlfriend's dad looked at my soft, nonathletic body and shrieked in shock and terror, "Drafted?! How the hell did this happen!?"

June 28, 1988

Mr. & Mrs. Denys Jones
76 Pusey Boulevard
Brantford, Ontario   N3R 2S5

Dear Mr. & Mrs. Jones:

On behalf of David Poile, our coaching staff and the entire Washington Capitals organization, I wanted to express our delight at selecting Keith in the recent Entry Draft.

We feel we are one of the most progressive and successful organizations in professional hockey and I want to assure you we stand ready to assist your son in every way possible as he pursues a hockey career as well as traveling down life's path.

As we tell every player selected, being drafted is an important and happy day, but it is only a brief moment in a career where success is determined by effort, determination and perseverance.

Keith has exhibited these "Capital Qualities" in his past performances which leaves us to believe that, along with his skill development, he has a tremendous chance for a successful career in the NHL and in particular with Washington.

We all look forward to a long and successful relationship and please be assured that all it takes is a phone call if I can ever be of assistance in any way to you or your son.

Sincerely,

Jack Button
Director of Player Personnel
and Recruitment

Bill Wilkinson

capital
centre

Landover, Maryland 20785   (301) 350-3400

The Capitals sent me this nice letter after I was drafted in 1988

CHAPTER 4

KNOWLEDGE IS GOOD

Once I accepted Bill Wilkinson's scholarship offer to attend Western Michigan University in Kalamazoo, I continued with my final year of junior hockey in Canada. During the tail end of the 1987-88 season in Niagara Falls, I injured my shoulder, but continued playing with the injury until the end of the season. I had a productive season and my final totals were 50-80-130 in 40 games.

I told my future college coach about my shoulder injury and he told me to drive down to Western Michigan so their doctors could take a look at it and devise a plan to rehabilitate it during the spring and summer of 1988. Then I would be ready for my freshman year in the fall with the Broncos. I would turn twenty in November of my freshman year of college.

I drove down to Western Michigan to meet with Coach Wilkinson and the trainer Bob "Hap" Zarzour. Bob's nickname is "Hap" because he is always smiling. (Hap is now the football trainer at Duke University and just a fantastic human being.)

So, we go into the trainer's room and they ask me to take my shirt off so they can take a look at my injured shoulder. Now, the coach has yet to see my "sculpted" physique and remember, I don't lift weights. I don't work out. I don't train. At all.

I take my shirt off and you wouldn't believe the looks on their faces as Coach and Hap scan down my unimpressive torso. I can still see the blank expressions on their stunned faces.

After seeing my soft, pasty, white torso, Coach Wilkinson blurts out in horror, "What are you doing?!" And then with a disgusted look,

Our western Michigan team photo.

"What is that?!" Wilkinson then asks me, "Have you ever been to the gym?" I answer, "Not really." He says, "You've got to take care of yourself!" I'm thinking he is going to revoke my scholarship any second now.

You would think this embarrassing episode with my new coach would motivate me to change my ways and hit the gym hard. It didn't.

You've got to remember, the bulk of my Junior hockey days are spent practicing once a week. We would just throw the pucks on the ice, and have some fun. I never played high level hockey in Canada growing up. Training wasn't a part of my culture. Plus, I took the summers off. No camps, no clinics, no power skating, no nothing. I mean nothing.

So, the summer going into my freshman year, I join a gym because I feel maybe this will get me going and ready for NCAA hockey. One day, I see fellow Brantfordite Paul Polillo at the gym. At this point, Paul has had two years of Western Michigan hockey under his belt. He just finished a strong sophomore season in which he scored 25 goals and had 60 assists (85 points) in 42 games. It ends up being Paul's best season at Western Michigan.

I ask Paul, "So, do you guys practice and train a lot at Western? He says, "Oh, no! It's nothing! Don't worry about it." I'm a little nervous about the physical toll it will take to play hockey at the next level after the way the coach looked at my body during my shoulder exam. I think maybe everyone has to be a world class, bodybuilding athlete. Paul eases my fears a bit, although I will find out later that he was deceiving me.

My workout routine remained the same. I would work out for a few days, get the normal muscle soreness, not push past that initial soreness, eat a burger, and go home. I went through the entire summer like this. I just couldn't get into the workout thing. I couldn't string consecutive good workouts together.

One day, I actually decided to go for a run. It was a nice summer day, so I took my shirt off as I ran through the streets of Brantford. I made my way to the gym for a rare workout. Finishing my fifteen-minute run, I arrived at the gym and walked inside. Since I was still hot and sweaty, I kept my shirt off. I truly didn't think anything of it. I don't have a self-conscious bone in my body. It's a good thing I don't.

I found an open space inside the gym and dropped down to do twenty push-ups. Then I stood up, with my gut hanging out, and proclaimed that my workout was finished. There were a lot of hockey players from Brantford in the gym and they must have been wondering, "Who is this clown?" I found out later that the whole gym was laughing as I left the building sweaty, shirtless, and abs-less.

A lot of people in Brantford didn't even know I played hockey. The hockey fraternity in town had a lot of Major Junior players and other guys I looked up to, and some of them didn't even know I existed. And to tell you the truth, that anonymity was kind of nice. People I went to school with didn't even know I played hockey. I wasn't the kind of jock at school that walks around like a big shot. I was nice to the cool kids and nice to the not-so-cool kids. I kind of floated around in the middle.

I barely did anything during the summer and soon it was time to head to college. I got to Western Michigan and the first thing we did as a team was some weight training in the gym to test everyone's strength.

Great. That's all I needed.

The initial weight training session gives the coaches a good idea of what everyone did during the off-season, how hard everyone trained, and where the freshman are strength-wise. The upperclassmen want to show their coaches and teammates how much stronger they got over the summer from all of their intense training. All of this is taking place at the big gym at Western Michigan.

Anyone who works out knows that when you bench press, most people start with the two big plates, the 45 pounders, to warm up. One on each side. The bar itself is 45 pounds. So when you add one 45 pound plate on each side you have 135 pounds total on the bar. It's a good weight that most male adults, especially Division 1 hockey players, use to warm up with. An average strength person can bench press ten to fifteen reps with 135 pounds. Rod Brind'Amour was probably benching 135 pounds thirty times while in college at Michigan State.

I'm not aware of this Weight Training 101 fact on this particular day because I have never bench-pressed with free weights before. Back home, I would do a few reps on the ole' rusty 1970s universal machines and call it a day. I was Mr. Universal 1988.

Anyway, everyone in the gym is pretty much sending this 135 pounds north at a pretty good pace. I'm feeling pretty strong, so I don't think much of it as I slide my body on the bench and under the bar. I'll crank maybe ten or so reps and sneak my way to the back of the room and call it a day.

I go to lift the 135 pounds up off the supports and I can't even get it off to start. Mike Eastwood is spotting me. Looking up, I see the look in his eyes and he knows I'm in trouble here with this elementary weight. Thank God, Mike is not a jerk and doesn't announce to the room that Olive Oyl here can't even do one rep. So, I look at Mike and say, "Man, that's kind of embarrassing."

Eastwood says, "Don't worry, that was me last year."

And that's what Western Michigan was all about – getting the late bloomer and intangible guys. Michigan State had the Rod Brind'Amours who were already in peak physical shape. Western got raw players like me and Mike Eastwood. Despite our "weaknesses," me and "Easty" would be the only two skaters who would go on to have decent NHL careers from this Western Michigan team.

My first year at Western Michigan was tough. I was tired all the time and I wanted to go home. I called and talked to one of my Junior B coaches, Mark Botel, a lot during my freshman year. Mark played 32 games in the NHL for the Flyers during the 1981-82 season.

Over the phone, Mark told me to hang in there and keep pushing. He knew how close he came to having a longer NHL career. He saw a potential in me that he believed might give me the chance. Mark told me to suck it up and stay at Western. Don't give up. He was another person who saw something in me that I didn't see in myself. I really wanted to go home at that point and I had to be convinced not to.

I was in pain every day. My skinny little legs were aching as they slowly gained some muscle. I was chubby, and I was miserable. That's no way to go through life.

For the most part, during my freshman year I just go home, curl up in my bed, and pass out in pain. I very rarely go out. It takes every ounce of energy to get through the day.

At this point, I have spent the past nineteen years of my life eating crap for food. I have the worst diet imaginable. I never eat healthy, never train, and here I am playing Division 1 hockey. I feel like I have to catch up for nineteen years of bad preparation. In fact, I play catch-up my entire career because I sometimes fall back into my old habits of cheese, bacon, chicken wings, and Budweiser — Jonesy's four basic food groups. My freshman year at Western Michigan I score 9 goals in 37 aching, painful games.

Through the natural maturation of my late-blooming body, and the rigors of Division 1 hockey, I slowly began getting stronger and more productive at Western. My goal total during my sophomore year increased to 19. That was a tie for fourth on the team with my Brantford buddy Paul Polillo.

Then as a junior, I scored 30 goals to lead the team while Mike Eastwood led the team in points. Eastwood then graduated and headed off to play professional hockey with the St. John's Maple Leafs in the AHL. He got a quick cup of coffee with the Toronto Maple Leafs in his first pro season, and went on to play 783 NHL games.

With Mike gone, I led the team in scoring my senior year by a 16-point margin. I scored 25 goals and dished out a college-career-high 31 assists.

I always had a nose for the net and that slowly began to show at Western Michigan. My Junior B coach, Terry Masterson, always called me a "hound dog." But, sometimes I had a hard time getting to the net because I just wasn't strong enough and I got knocked down a lot on my way there.

I was maturing and growing stronger just by being involved in the daily grind of Division 1 College Hockey. All of the skating, the eating, and the workouts were having the desired effect. I also began to work out a little bit more during the summer months back home. Following my freshman year I began to work out with a couple of older guys in Brantford.

Chris Pusey was a goaltender who was three years older than me and just wrapping up a brief pro career. Everyone called him "Puse" – rhymes with fuse. He's the "Moonlight" Graham of Brantford, the player in the movie *Field of Dreams* who played in just one Major League Baseball game.

On October 19, 1985, Puse appeared in his first and only NHL game. He was brought in to start the second period with his Red Wings losing. He was 3-3 in save chances in the second period. If the Red Wings could come from behind, he would get an NHL win. In the third period, the Blackhawk's Marc Bergevin scored his first NHL goal off Pusey, while Eddie Olczyk and Curt Fraser end any chance of a Red Wing comeback and a Pusey win. During that game, the Blackhawks score on Puse with a shot which is later used in an instructional video on "How to score on a breakaway." I never let Chris forget about that. "Puse" returned to Adirondack the week after his one NHL appearance. Later, during my NHL career, I Fed Exed "Puse" two used tickets, my NHL pay stub, and a note that read, "This could have been you." He didn't find it very amusing.

After my freshman year ended, I came home to Brantford and Chris took me under his wing. Chris had become a physical fitness nut and I was one of his students now. In the same gym that I walked into with no shirt on, Chris said, "You're with me." He began to push me as best as he could to get me stronger, and we slowly put a little muscle on this chicken body.

Along with Chris, another guy from Brantford named Doug Brown, who played some minor league hockey, took me in as well. Those guys were a little bit older and I looked up to them. The three of us became great friends because of how hard they pushed me to get stronger and become a better player on the ice.

We ran a lot and I went from running three miles in twenty-seven minutes to running three miles in eighteen minutes. I can run because I'm so long-legged and bowlegged, and I begin to surpass Doug and Chris despite the fact they have been training for five years and I have been training for five minutes. I can get a second wind and go and go and go. We raced and competed and really pushed each other. I owe them so much for how they were able to motivate me to do at least an acceptable level of physical training.

While running, I would say in my mind, "1.8, 1.8, 1.8." I said that because Kelly Miller just signed a contract to make 1.8 million a year to play with the Washington Capitals. I didn't know Kelly Miller. But, since I was drafted by the Capitals, I sort of looked at Kelly Miller as the kind of NHL player I could maybe be. And maybe I could someday get that kind of paycheck. "1.8, 1.8, 1.8."

Kelly Miller went to Michigan State and we kind of had similar NCAA careers. I was like, "I can't believe someone like that can make that kind of money!"

"1.8, 1.8, 1.8."

This would turn out to be the most money I made in the NHL.

My summer training made me stronger and the added muscle raises my weight from 177 to 190 pounds. I did enough to just get by physically. I probably should have run six miles after mastering three. Three miles in eighteen minutes is good, I'll stay there, I said.

I would go to the gym and do a few sets of everything in about an hour and fifteen minutes, and then I'd see you tomorrow. It was more than I ever had done, but it's about what your average banker does at your local gym. I never went above and beyond while training, but it nonetheless paid dividends in the way I played on the ice the rest of my college career. And once the season started I scaled way back. I was the guy in the back of the weight room, skipping sets and cracking jokes.

Despite my off-ice work ethic, which may not have always been conducted at full throttle, I always had the ability to show up for the game. I always gave it my all on the ice and so coaches gave me leniency for my off-ice ethic. I was the classic game player. Some are practice players and some are gamers. I'm a gamer. I know I have physical limitations that either I put on myself or are just there. I'm not sure which one it is. I know I only have so much in the tank, but I'll give all that's in there.

My four-year hockey education was now up. Western Michigan was a great experience. It's where I met my wife, Laura. I grew as a hockey player so much that I signed with the Washington Capitals after our college playoffs. That was unbelievable. I left school immediately and headed to Baltimore to begin my professional hockey career with the AHL Baltimore Skipjacks.

From Junior C, to a year of Junior B, to almost quitting early in my college career, and now to this? My unlikely road to the NHL continued forward.

The year was 1992 and I was twenty-three years old.

My Freshman year at Western Michigan University.

CHAPTER 5

"ARE YOU GOING TO JUST SIT THERE OR ARE YOU GOING TO FIGHT HIM FOR IT?"

My college years came to an end and I was off to begin my professional hockey career with the Baltimore Skipjacks of the American Hockey League in the spring of 1992.

The Skipjacks season was just about over so I ended up playing just six games. The Capitals organization just wanted us prospects to get our feet wet. The Caps wanted us to use this end-of-the-season cup of AHL coffee as our pro hockey orientation.

Me, Pat Peake, Steve Konowalchuk, Jason Wooley, and John Slaney all arrived at the tail end of that 1991-92 season. Byron Dafoe and Olaf Kolzig were the goalies when we arrived in Baltimore and Kolzig just couldn't buy a win. And it's driving Ollie crazy.

Kolzig had lost an AHL record seventeen straight games and was losing his freaking mind. It's unbelievable how crazy this twenty-two-year-old kid was. As we all know, Ollie turned out to be one of the great guys in hockey. But that season in Baltimore, he goes 5-17-2. Because of a glut of goalies in the Capitals system, G.M. David Poile wanted both Kolzig and Dafoe to play, so he loaned Ollie to Rochester. Well, Ollie took Rochester to the final after going 25-16-4. Rochester lost to Cape Breton in the Calder Cup final. "Zilla's" career really took off from there. He took the Capitals to the Stanley Cup Final five years later, and became the face of the franchise.

I ended up scoring two goals and getting four assists in my six game-end-of-the-season cup of coffee with the Skipjacks. Unfortunately, the Skipjacks finished last in the division and hold the second fewest points in the AHL in 1991-92, so we didn't qualify for the playoffs.

Just before the 1992 Stanley Cup playoffs were set to start, the NHL players go on strike for the first time in NHL history.

Players walked off the job on April 1 and returned April 11 after the NHL and NHLPA agreed to a two-year contract. The 30 games that were supposed to be played during the strike were rescheduled and no games were missed. This was Bob Goodenow's first year as head of the union. The players demanded full control of the marketing rights to their images. This included the use of player pictures on trading cards, posters, and other merchandise. The playoff money fund for players increased from $3.2 million to $7.5 million.

I go back to Kalamazoo, Michigan during the short strike and do nothing. The strike gets resolved and the Capitals call me and the other "young guns" back up to be part of the Black Aces. The Black Aces were the emergency group of players who kept skating during the playoffs, bag skating they called it, just in case there was a rash of injuries and a spare body was needed to fill out the roster. One that was in shape. The chances of actually playing were beyond remote.

Because we needed someone to skate us, the Caps brought up our Baltimore coach Barry Trotz, as well. We skated after the Capitals had their regular practice. No one knew who the hell we were. Naturally, Barry wanted to make an impression on the Capitals brass casually watching from above, and so he pushed us relentlessly.

All of that skating was exhausting. But it was kind of cool when we got to the Capitals' first playoff game against the Penguins at home and we saw our names on the scratch list. And then we got to travel with the team to Pittsburgh on the team plane and stay in a real nice hotel. But all of that skating was killing me. I hated it. And for some reason, I stopped drinking water while skating during that phase of my life. I have no idea what I was thinking with that liquid strike. I was always trying to lose weight back then, or get in better shape, and I thought not drinking water would help. It's unbelievable my organs didn't shut down. I felt awful from all the skating and the lack of water. And I distinctly remember feeling unsure whether I could keep up with this grueling regimen. I'm not sure if I can keep doing this.

Well, on April 25, 1992, the Capitals beat the Penguins 7-2 to go up three games to one in the opening round of the playoffs and I'm pissed. Sure, we're winning, but there's no sign of the skating coming to an end. The longer the Capitals play, the longer I'm skating!

So, we're flying back to Washington up three games to one and I turn to Steve Konowalchuk and say, "This sucks. These guys are going to win the Stanley Cup. We're going to be bag skating for two more months."

The Penguins decide to make some adjustments for Game 5 and play a little more defensively. Pittsburgh scores the go-ahead goal and I look over at Steve and give him a thumbs up, "Yeah, baby!" I'm rooting for my team to blow a 3-1 series lead because I'm so tired of all this skating. Meanwhile, Konowalchuk looks at me like I'm some kind of asshole.

The Penguins win Game 5 and Game 6. With each goal I'm giving Konowalchuk a low five under the seat and he's getting more and more pissed off at me. Amazingly, the Penguins win Game 7 and win the series, coming back from a three games to one deficit. Eventually, they go on to win their second straight Stanley Cup.

To this day, I believe I cursed myself by rooting for the Capitals to lose that series to the Penguins so I wouldn't have to keep skating. I'm the only player in NHL history to be on three different teams that all blew 3-1 series leads: The Capitals, Avalanches, and the Flyers. Amazing.

With the season over, I headed back to Kalamazoo for the summer, still not drinking water while exerting myself. I started this at the end of my senior year at Western Michigan and for some reason stuck with it. All summer long I felt awful and thought something was wrong. This won't be the first time that my mind plays tricks on me with regards to my health.

After doing all of that training during my college years, especially the last summer before my senior year, I went back to doing nothing. You would think with the first NHL training camp on the horizon, I would be training like Rocky. Nope.

The previous couple of summers while attending college I didn't do much moving of heavy items for the company my girlfriend's family ran. I couldn't risk an injury to my back and I had to find a safer way to make money. So, I decided to mow grass for the Board of Education. I had my own mower that I rode around town from field to field or wherever mowing was needed. It was a two-and-a-half day job that you got paid five days to do. Typical city job. I'd get the grass done in two-and-a-half days. On the fourth and fifth days I'd drive to Kenny Wilson's house, park the mower in his garage, and play Nintendo baseball all day long while on the clock. This went on all summer. Now, since I was a college kid, they didn't take any taxes out of my paycheck. I thought that was how all paychecks worked.

My first automobile, a Mitsubishi 3000 twin turbo,
I pretty much blew my signing bonus on that beauty!

Well, the summer after my Baltimore Skipjack cup of coffee and first Stanley Cup playoff experience, I got my signing bonus of $75,000, so I didn't have to mow lawns anymore. In fact I spent the summer in Kalamazoo playing big man on campus as I got set to attend my first NHL training camp. There were no taxes taken out of my signing bonus and it never dawned on me that I would have to pay taxes down the road. Just call me H&R Blockhead.

I immediately began spending the $75,000 bonus money. I went out and bought a red Mitsubishi 3000 Twin Turbo sports car for $40,000. I didn't even know how to drive it because I had never driven a stick shift before. I sat in the back seat while our trainer "Hap" Zarzour test drove it for me. "How do you like it?" I asked. Hap says, "Great! We'll take it!"

I ended up wearing the clutch out after only 25,000 miles. I drove it into a dealership with one gear left. The guy at the dealership couldn't believe it. He asks, "Was it making a noise or anything?" Was it making a noise?! I got one gear left here! Luckily, it was under warranty.

I took the remainder of the bonus money and went to Las Vegas. In no time the entire bonus check was gone. Like I said, I wasn't used to taxes coming out of my paycheck. I spent more money than I had taken in, and in no time I am flat broke. I literally had to borrow money from my sister Carolyn to go to training camp in September.

I signed a two-way contract that paid me $35,000 if I played in Baltimore and $140,000 if I made the NHL. I had gone to camp broke, and I had just borrowed money off my sister. Plus, I had this expensive car to take care of. I had to make the team! I had no choice.

Meanwhile, I weighed 218 pounds when I headed to Capitals Camp. Fat and poor. They gave me number 41 when I arrived at training camp, which is not a good sign. Steve Konowalchuk had number 22 and Pat Peake was like number 11. I'm thinking I have no shot of making the team with this number. Especially after not lifting a single weight that summer on account of not feeling well due to the whole water denial thing. I'm convinced I have something bad going on inside me at this point, but keep my health issue to myself.

The only bit of training I did all summer was one jog around a soccer field. I figured I should do something before training camp. I found a local soccer field in Kalamazoo, ran around the field once, stopped, turned to my buddy and said, "That's it. Let's go eat a pizza."

So, to prepare for my first NHL training camp I jog one lap around a soccer field.

I got to camp and I was a mess health-wise, probably from my lack of water, my nerves, and my mounting debt. The Capitals sent me out to get a bunch of tests to see why I wasn't not feeling well. It was probably also a mental thing, from not working out at all. I needed an excuse to tell them why I couldn't train.

So, the doctors find this small polyp in my stomach and laser it out. It's not a big deal, but I can blame my summer of sloth on a stomach polyp. "That's why I'm fat, Coach!" Perfect.

Training camp got underway and the Capitals started testing us. They test my fat percentage and I'm like 18.5 percent. Our top-notch guys had like 6 percent. Obviously, I was out of shape.

Then we hit the ice and Terry Murray wanted us to skate to test our conditioning. Three laps one way, rest for forty-five seconds, and then three laps the other way for time. I skate my first three laps in forty-two seconds. Most guys are doing it in thirty-six seconds, so I'm not too far off. I rest for forty-five seconds and then start my three laps in the opposite direction. Now, I haven't skated all summer and my legs lock up. It takes me fifty-seven seconds to go three laps. They wanted a two-second difference at most. I was at fifteen.

How much did I not look like an NHL player with that soft body of mine? Well, on the first day of training camp I was sitting in the locker room and Michael Pivonka, about to start his seventh year in the NHL, says to me, "Hey kid, can you grab my sticks for me?"

I'm a little taken aback by this request, but then I'm thinking that it must be a rookie thing so I go and grab Pivonka's sticks for him. No big deal.

Well, later on in training camp, once new faces start to get recognizable and us white guys all don't look alike, Peter Bondra comes up to me and says, "Hey Jonesy. Remember that time Pivonka told you to get him his sticks?"

I say, "Yeah. What was that all about? I haven't seen any other rookies get any vets their sticks for them."

Bondra replies, "Your body is so bad Pivonka said he thought there was no way you were a player. He thought you were the equipment guy!"

Preseason games were set to start and I was still stressing economically. I'm in such poor condition and I needed to make the team to pay my sister back, take care of my car, and have some financial freedom. At the very least, I began to feel a little better on the ice since I'd resumed drinking water. That strange and flawed experiment with not drinking water while on the ice in practices and games had ended.

We went to Ottawa for a home and home preseason thing they call the Capital Cup. I scored my first goal in an NHL uniform in that OIC preseason game. I was out with Al Iafrate after the first game because I wasn't not supposed to play in the second game. Al liked to hang around with the young guys. He was very generous and would take care of drinks and food for the guys just getting started. We called him the human highlight film.

We were hanging out in the mall after going out the night before and I was just sitting eating a big bucket of Kentucky Fried Chicken. Just chowing it down like a hungry dog on the back of a chicken truck. Around noon, I get a page all of a sudden. I call about the page with my greasy fingers and the message is from the coach. Terry Murray tells me I need to play later that day. This after just devouring an entire bucket of chicken! I got to tell ya, I had a higher opinion of the

NHL. Imagine getting paged in the middle of the mall, while eating fried chicken, to tell you that you had to play in the NHL game that night. Needless to say I didn't move too well on the ice. Ironically, I won my only cup that night. The Capital Cup.

We headed back to Washington for the final stretch of training camp and we were getting down to the nitty-gritty in terms of who made the Capitals and who got sent back down to Baltimore and the minor leagues. With my mounting debt and a salary difference of almost $100,000 between playing in the AHL and NHL, I resorted to what first became a strength when I played my last season of Junior B. Sensing an opening, a gap in the overall quality of a hockey team, I squirm my way in to fill that need through street smarts, sheer will, and desperation. On this team, I saw there was a need for a guy willing to fight.

Dale Hunter came to me early in training camp and said, "You got to look at it this way in hockey. You are sitting in your kitchen with $500,000 on the table. Someone walks into your home, scoops up all the money in his arms, and begins to walk out of your house with you sitting there. Are you going to let him just walk out with the half million or are you going to fight him for it?" I say to Hunter, "I fight him for it!" And Dale says, "That's how you have to approach making the team."

I didn't want to make the 1992-93 Washington Capitals as a fourth line guy who had to fight and got little ice time. I pictured myself as a different kind of player. But, in order to get my foot in the door and start the process I had to adapt myself to that role to make the team. I understood the situation enough to say, this is what I'm going to do. I'm going to start to fight and give them the best fourth-line-type player in camp.

So, I start to fight and I get pounded a couple of times. I am so out of shape that I have to do something. I fight Brent Hughes who is trying to make the Bruins, and Steve Leach who used to play for the Capitals, but by this time was an established player with the Bruins. I have a couple of more fights as I'm trying to fill this role and make the team. And get that NHL salary.

Now, fighting wasn't second nature for me. Believe it or not, I was a spectator for most of those Junior C brawls and never had a fight in my college career. But, I had to map out a way to make the team and pay back my sister. Despite the incredibly awful shape I was in physically, I felt I had done enough, through fighting, to make the team.

As training camp wound down I was getting in better shape. The one good thing about my genetics is that I can get into (and out of) shape very quickly. Never ideal shape, but no one was asking me to get their sticks anymore!

I have a lot of inner drive that comes out at desperate times. By the end of training camp I wasn't just hoping to make the team. I felt I deserved to make it. There was no doubt about it in my mind.

Besides the financial drive to make the 1992-93 Capitals, there was actually a bigger drive as I looked at the schedule for the upcoming regular season. The first game was in Toronto against the Leafs in Maple Leaf Gardens. What a way to cap off an amazing road to the NHL but to play in front of the people I had sat with as a fan just a few years before. I wanted to play in front of Walter Scott and my ex-girlfriend, and all those people who saw me riding around town on my mower, and maybe some of the people who were in that Brantford gym when I walked in without my shirt on, did my push-ups, and left. I wanted to look up at the crowd and give a little parade wave with a smirky smile as if to say, "Hey, everybody, what's up?"

It would have meant everything to me to play in that game in Toronto on opening night. I mean, you never really know if you can really play in the NHL. I played well in college. I played pretty well in my quick cup of coffee with Baltimore the previous spring. But could I play in the NHL? I really didn't know. It was dangling right there in front of me. Also, if I was only going to play in one NHL game, I wanted it to be against the Toronto Maple Leafs in Maple Leaf

Gardens. If I wasn't good enough to play in the NHL, I could have accepted that. But, I would always be able to say that I played one NHL game and I played it in Maple Leaf Gardens. I made the show.

So, training camp was winding down and us guys on the fringe of the roster were stressing over whether we would make the team or be sent down to the minors. Everyone's nerves were frazzled.

Well, it's time for me to hear the verdict handed down by the Washington Capitals. Would I make the team or not? G.M. David Poile calls me into a makeshift room with all of his scouting and administrative staff sitting around this big table at our practice rink.

Mr. Poile says, "Keith, you've had a nice training camp, but we're sending you to Baltimore." In front of this big room of people, I respond, "You're making a big mistake."

And then I let loose on them, "You know I made this team. The players know I made this team. I know I made this team. But I'll go down to the minors. And I'll be back in two weeks to play in the NHL. And you won't regret it when I come back."

The room was silent. This was an out-of-shape, seventh round draft pick talking here.

My incentive to make this bold proclamation was that I really wanted to play in that game in Toronto on opening night in front of all those people who grew up watching me make a fool of myself. Look at me now!

I believed what I said to Mr. Poile and company, but I was also selling myself. I knew the one chance I had to play in the Toronto game was to throw it at them like that and maybe they'd change their minds or something. It didn't work. I headed down to Baltimore and the AHL while the Capitals flew to Toronto for the start of the NHL season.

Years later, Terry Murray, then the Capitals head coach, tells me that following the meeting where I stated my NHL case, David Poile told Murray, "I just met the future captain of the Washington Capitals."

"Really? Who is that?" Murray replied.

And Poile tells him, "Keith Jones!"

Murray then says, despite having just been behind the bench for six of my preseason games, "Keith Jones? Who's he?"

As I headed for Baltimore, the Capitals ended up beating the Maple Leafs in Toronto, in front of Walter Scott and a disappointed Maple Leaf Gardens.

CHAPTER 6
"I'M MINUS 7!"

Having failed to make the Capitals following my first NHL training camp, I began the 1992-93 hockey season in the AHL in what
turned out to be Baltimore Skipjacks final year of existence. The franchise moved to Portland the following season and became the Pirates.
Led by Michel Picard, Jeff Nelson, Mike Boback, and yes, our boy Olaf
Kolzig in the net, the Pirates won the Calder Cup their first season
in Maine. I was really happy for Olie, especially having seen firsthand
what he went through in the spring of '92.

The very next day after Capitals G.M. David Poile sent me down
to the minors, we played the Hershey Bears. I went out and scored
four goals in the opening night game, despite still being a bit out of
shape after my summer training routine of one lap around a soccer
field followed by a medium cheese pizza. I wanted to send a message
to David Poile, Terry Murray, and the Capitals brass. Training camp
with the Caps had at least put me in passable physical condition, although I still had the body of a TV repairman.

I got off to a good start playing for head coach Barry Trotz and
the Skipjacks. In my first eight games in Baltimore, I scored seven goals
and dished out three assists for ten points. This only made my patience
for reaching the NHL thinner. I had to get there and I had to get there
right now. The accelerator in the car was being pushed to the floor.

Meanwhile, the Capitals were getting hammered with injuries
and some underachieving play. They were off to a poor start under
head coach Terry Murray and after nine games their record was 3-6.
So, they decide to call up Steve Konowalchuk, who was on the Skipjacks roster with me in Baltimore.

Steve is four years younger than me and was a third-round pick. He scored 50 goals for the Portland Winter Hawks in the Western Hockey League when he was twenty years old. I was coming off a season of Junior B at age twenty when I was drafted. I think they saw Steve as the better prospect. But, being twenty-four years old at the time I thought I could help the Capitals maybe a little more.

I flipped out at the decision to bring up Kono over me. I go to Barry Trotz and say, "You guys are assholes. You're making a mistake. I should be the guy getting called up!" I was livid. I was so desperate to make it to the NHL, and knowing I was so close only made it harder. To say nothing of the fact I had bills to pay!.

I was running on empty as I tried to get my body into professional hockey shape. At that point, all I wanted was to taste the NHL. If it was one game, it was one game. Maybe I wasn't cut out for that life anyway, I thought. Maybe it was too strenuous and I wasn't genetically cut out for it. But, I wanted to get up and play in at least one game as quickly as possible. I pushed myself, the coaching staff, and the management to get me up to the Capitals to play. I was relentless.

As it turns out, Steve Konowalchuk didn't get called up to the NHL just yet, and he ended up playing the eighth game of the year in the AHL season with us in Baltimore. We are playing Utica and we're losing 9-8 late in the third period. We pull our goalie as we try to get the tying goal. Well, Utica gets control of the puck and sends the puck down the ice at the empty net. The horn goes off just before the puck crosses the line. By rule, the entire puck has to cross the line before the horn goes off for the goal to count. This isn't basketball. That's no goal!

I'm on the ice at the time and the officials erroneously allow the goal to stand. This means that not only do we lose 10-8, but also that all of the players on the ice at the time of the goal, including me, get a minus on the statistical sheet. Normally, who cares? A loss is a loss and we lose 10-8. Who cares? I do.

I start chasing the referee around the ice saying, "How in the **** can you count that goal? The ****ing buzzer went off before the puck crossed the line!"

The referee is looking at me like I have two heads and four boogers hanging out of my four nostrils. He's like, "Dude, the game is over. What do you care?"

One of our assistants, Paul Gardner, comes over and says, "Jonesy, what are you doing?"

I reply, "That ****ing buzzer went off before the puck crossed the line! That's no goal!"

Gardner says, "Why do you care? The game is over!"

I go, "I'm ****ing minus 7!"

Paul Gardner says, "What?"

I say, "I'm minus 7!"

We lose 10-8.

I scored two goals on the power play that night, but during a power play, it doesn't count as a plus for the players on the ice whose team scored. You do, however, get a minus if the other team scores a shorthanded goal against you, which happened twice during this game to me. Otherwise, to quote Austin Powers, it was "pretty standard stuff really." You get a plus when you are on the ice and your team scores a goal and you get a minus when you are on the ice and the other team scores.

So, I repeat to Paul Gardner, "I'm a ****ing minus 7!" which, mind you, has to be close to an AHL record.

The next day we're having a meeting and coach Trotz addresses the team. He says, "Guys, there was a guy on our team who was a minus 7 on the stats sheet last night against Utica. I'm going to show you guys all of the goals on the video and I want to show you something about hockey."

Barry, of course, is talking about me. He shows all seven goals scored while I was on the ice. He shows the tape, stops, and says,

"Jonesy had his man on every goal."

I was in the right position for every goal and I was a minus 7.

Later that night, after Barry Trotz acquitted me of all crimes in my minus 7 game against Utica, I was at my apartment listening to the Capitals game on the radio. I was sharing a place with Skipjack teammates Trevor Halverson and Rob Leask in Odenton, Maryland, halfway between Baltimore and Washington. On that night, I didn't want them to know what I was doing.

I went upstairs to the loft in the apartment where I was staying, and into this little cubby hole to listen to the Capitals late night game against the Vancouver Canucks on my Sony Walkman radio. That is how obsessed I was with getting to the NHL. There I was, thinking that something could happen at any moment that would trigger a series of events that would get me to the NHL. The Capitals were 3-6 as they went into Vancouver to play the Canucks that night, so maybe there wouldn't even need to be an injury for me to get called up to the big time. They were struggling and maybe ready to make some changes.

I was listening to the game with my headphones so my roommates would think I was listening to music and not the game. I knew Konowalchuk was about to get called up at any moment, so I thought I might be next if someone got injured or if the Caps lost another game. I knew it was a critical time in their season. Going into the third period against Vancouver, nothing really newsworthy had happened yet.

Now before the season, the Capitals traded Dino Ciccarelli for Kevin Miller, Kelly's brother, which, incidentally, gave us Miller brothers and Hunter brothers. Anyway, Ciccarelli was coming off a 38-goal season and another productive playoff series for the Caps. He went on to score 41 goals for the Red Wings the year after Washington traded him. Meanwhile, Kevin Miller had zero goals in his first ten Washington games, and the Capitals were now trying to cut bait and deal him. I, of course, saw this as my opening to getting called up.

I continued listening to the game on my Walkman radio. Early in the third period, Kevin Miller took a spearing penalty and was ejected from the game. I said to myself, "OK, here we go. This will put him deeper in the doghouse."

Then, moments later, Mark Hunter takes a big hit in Vancouver that sounds bad even on the radio in Maryland. The hit gives Hunter a concussion that not only knocks him out of the lineup, but eventually ends his career. He never played another NHL game.

With about ten minutes left in the third period, my roommate, Ron Leask, taps me on the shoulder. He thinks I'm listening to a CD or something.

As I'm listening to the game, the phone rings, but I don't hear it. Rob says, "The phone is for you. It's Poile."

I pick up the phone and Poile says, "Keith, you have a 6:00 a.m. flight to Calgary tomorrow. Get yourself ready. You're coming to the NHL."

I about poop my pants. I've made the show.

Well, I went to the airport the next morning and there was Steve Konowalchuk on the same flight as me. Kevin Miller was three days away from being traded to St. Louis for defenseman Paul Cavallini, so there was an opening for a winger on the team. Add the injury to Mark Hunter and that made two openings. I had my opening, Kono had his opening, and it was time to take advantage of opportunity knocking. We were off to Alberta to join the team on the road.

We arrived late in Calgary, got a decent night's sleep, and then got up the next day for the morning skate. We finished the morning skate, but didn't know if we were going to play that night against the Flames. Head coach Terry Murray, like a lot of coaches will do when dealing with young players, didn't tell us if we were going to play that night. He didn't want us to worry about it all day.

All afternoon I was saying to myself over and over, "This could be it." I was so excited and fired up to play in an NHL game. I remember thinking, "It's a miracle I'm here and now it is so close. I can't believe it."

Kono and I went to the rink after a quality power nap and, sure enough, we were both in the lineup against the Calgary Flames. October 30, 1992. And when I think about it now, October 30 was the perfect date for me to make my NHL debut.

October 30 is "Devil's Night," a tradition in Detroit that goes back about seventy-five years. Traditionally, teenagers in the Detroit area engage in a night of mischievous behavior, which usually consists of acts of minor vandalism, like egging the homes of neighbors or throwing rolls of toilet paper in trees. This is done in retaliation for "real or perceived wrongs," or simply done as a prank. It got out of hand as Detroit teens went from egging homes to setting them on fire in the 1970s and 80s. What a leap! My "Devil's Night" would be relived on a nightly basis in the NHL with elbows, crosschecks, high sticks, and slew foots. October 30 kind of made it feel like I had made a deal with the devil.

I walked into the dressing room and saw my Capitals jersey, with JONES on the back, hanging in my stall. I put it on as I was getting dressed for the warm-up. I'll never forget putting that jersey on in the visiting dressing room in Calgary and staring at myself in the mirror. I tried hard not to be seen by anyone as I stood there shaking my head and looking at myself in the mirror wearing an NHL game jersey. It wouldn't have been very cool to have been seen doing this. But I was in an absolutely euphoric state because I was about to play in my first NHL game.

I hit the ice for the warm-up and bumped into everybody and everything as I stared around the Saddledome. I couldn't take a pass or get a good shot off during the warm-up, and I felt like I was having a stroke as I skated around in complete shock at being on NHL ice during a regular season game.

While it was apropos to be making my debut on "Devil's Night," it was also apropos that on my first shift, I got a penalty while playing on the fourth line with Jeff Greenlaw and Alan May. Later in the game, I bumped into Calgary's Gary Roberts in front of our bench. There we were, lining up for the ensuing face-off, when Terry Murray leans over and screams, "Try him Roberts, he'll kick your ass!!"

I then say to Roberts, "I swear he's not talking about me."

Thank God, Roberts believed me. Murray thought I was a fighter because I fought so much in the preseason trying to make the team. I went on to have twenty-five fighting majors, one win, and twenty-four ties. Thankfully, Joe Sacco couldn't fight either. We won my first NHL game in Calgary 3-1. I was 1-0. I should have retired.

My undefeated career didn't last long as we lost the next night, Halloween Night, 4-2. During that game, I got a chance to play with Dale Hunter.

After the loss to the Oilers that night, Huntsy took me out for a beer at a place called Barry T's in Edmonton. Now, keep in mind I had just kind of taken his brother Mark's roster spot. You wouldn't think he would want to have much to do with me. Well, we were sitting there having a beer and Dale says, "Jonesy, you are going to be a good player in the NHL. You belong here. Just continue to work hard and you are going to have a nice career."

It was amazing hearing words like that come from someone that I had watched play for so many years and looked up to. You can't over-value the impact words like that have on a young player. Obviously, the words gave me confidence and inspired me. We had two days off until our next game. On November 3, 1992 we played a neutral site game in Indianapolis, Indiana against the Chicago Blackhawks.

Indianapolis is where Wayne Gretzky, also from Brantford, began his professional career in the WHA in the fall of 1978. Wayne only played eight games for the Indianapolis Racers before he was sold to the Edmonton Oilers, also of the WHA at the time. At the end of that season, on March 22, 1979, the Edmonton Oilers, New England Whalers (who became the Hartford Whalers), Quebec Nordiques, and Winnipeg Jets joined the NHL as expansion teams, and the WHA ceased operations.

On November 3, 1992, in the Hoosier state, I scored my first goal in the National Hockey League. Indianapolis is driving distance from Kalamazoo, so my buddy Louie Nisker, the guy I took the lap around the soccer field with over the summer, came down to see me play. So, I'm skating on the ice during the warm-up without a helmet so I can look my coolest, and as I'm skating around feeling cool, Louie leans over the glass, waves, and screams, "Hey Jonesy!!"

I look over to see who it is and at the same time I step on a stray puck. I proceed to trip, fall, and slam into the boards. A great start in Market Square Arena.

The game started and Ed Belfour is in the net for Chicago. Belfour had a great year in 1992-93. He went on to win 41 games, second most in his career, and had seven shutouts. The Blackhawks, as a whole, were a good team that year. They went on to win 106 points to lead the Western Conference. They had Jeremy Roenick, who scored 50 goals, Chris Chelios, and Steve Larmer. They were a really good team.

In my first shift, I went out and scored a typical garbage goal for my first in the NHL. The puck is on a plaque in my basement in New Jersey today. Like Wayne Gretzky, my first NHL point came against the Chicago Blackhawks. Gretzky got his on an assist in his first NHL game. Gretzky's first NHL goal came against the Canucks in his second game. Both Wayne and I got our first NHL goals on backhanders. Yes, the comparisons between Wayne Gretzky and I are endless.

I went on to get a couple of assists against Chicago that night as well. All this while my buddy Louie ate seven pieces of pizza in the stands cheering me on.

My friend Randy Robles, of Elias Sports Bureau, who works with me at Versus, researched and found that of the 6,000 NHL players who have scored an NHL goal, I'm the only player in NHL history to score his first NHL goal at a neutral site game. Therefore, I have no team logo on my first NHL goal puck. Just the NHL symbol.

We went on to beat the Blackhawks 4-1 in Indianapolis. After the game I said to myself, "There must be another league. How in the hell can I get three points in the NHL?"

That humility would serve me well in situations where I might otherwise have gotten my clock cleaned. Later on in my rookie year, we headed to the Spectrum in Philadelphia and I was pretty nervous. I mean, it was the Spectrum, it was Philadelphia, and the fans, then as now, were right on top of you.

Keith Acton was the classic pest/rat for the Flyers at the time. This is at the tail end of his career, so he had learned plenty of material during a long NHL tenure that would eventually span 1,023 games. If you didn't know, Acton has great one liners, he's hilarious, full of energy and a hell of a hockey player. Well, during the warmup of that Capital-Flyers matchup, we were just verbally abusing each other as we circled around the red line. It was like a Friars Club Roast, and Acton and I were roasting each other. This barrage of putdowns and one liners went on the entire game. Finally, in the third period, Dave Brown had had enough.

Dave Brown was a 6'5" 205 pound brawler from Saskatoon, Saskatchewan. Once, when he was asked about his chances of ever winning the NHL's Lady Byng Trophy, he replied that he would only win the trophy, "if they renamed it the Man Byng Trophy." Great line.

Anyway, Brown comes on the ice after about the 700th exchange between me and Keith Acton. Brown stands next to me. Looking down at me he says, "Jonesy, if you don't shut the f★★★ up, I'm going to kick your ass."

To which I replied, "Yes, sir, Mr. Brown. No problem!"

You see, a smart pest survives. A dumb pest gets his ass kicked. I was there to score some goals, agitate, and survive.

CHAPTER 7

"I'D LOVE TO GET TO PAUL MACDERMID MONEY. THAT MUST BE UNBELIEVABLE!"

After leaving Western Michigan, I had signed a three year, two way contract to play for the Capitals. The deal paid me that $75,000 bonus I blow in about five minutes on my Tracy Chapman fast car and a Vegas-baby vacation, in addition to my salary which was $140,000 for my first year in the NHL, $150,000 for the second, and $160,000 for the third. Nothing makes you more hungry or more desperate than a two way contract. Except maybe owing your sister money.

My agent at the time was one-eyed Gene McBurney, a multi-millionaire guy from Toronto. He had way more money than any of the players he represented. When I eventually fired him, he got a huge kick out of it. There was a clause in my first contract that said if I played fifty NHL games in any one of my first three seasons, the contract became a one way deal for the remainder of the deal. I would get the NHL rate whether I was in the NHL or not.

So, after I got called up to the Capitals for my first game in Calgary, I went on to play forty-nine straight games in the NHL with Washington. One more game and the $140,000 I was making remains my salary for the rest of the year, whether I am sent back down to the Skipjacks or not. It also meant that my salary the following year would be $150,000 whether I was in the NHL or AHL. This is a huge deal to a young, entry level player.

Well, into game fifty, Capitals coach Terry Murray pulls me aside and says, "You're not playing tonight." I'm pissed, but I don't say anything. Of course I know I'm one game away from the magical and lucrative fifty-game mark. And I know the Capitals know. The team is playing well and I'm playing well. This is bullshit. I know what is going on here.

So, I sit out the game against the Islanders and once again my brain starts to overwork. I'm obsessed now with the one way contract and I'm thinking, "Maybe I'll never play in another NHL game." I know what the one-way contract means and how once you get your foot in the door, what a nice room it is to be in. With more expansion on the horizon, I could really be around for awhile if I can establish myself and my role in the NHL. I sit out the game, go home, and get up the next day and head to practice.

Now, we have three days until our next game against the Bruins, so this is really playing with my mind! As I get inside the rink I see Terry Murray and say, "I better be playing tomorrow night!"

He says, "What do you mean?"

I say, "You know what my contract situation is!"

And he says incredulously, "I don't know anything about contracts, I don't know what you're talking about!"

And I say, "I know you know where my number is at!"

Murray responds, "I don't know what you are talking about. You're in there tomorrow night!"

I say, "OK, good."

I knew how the game worked. They wanted to make me think about it. To show the ultimate power they had over me. Anyway, so I wake up for game fifty and I'm doing everything VERY carefully. I mean, I am walking around the bathroom slowly to make sure I don't slip on a wet spot. I chew slowly and completely so I don't choke. I drive to the rink slowly, signaling when I change lanes and leaving plenty of distance between me and the car in front of me. I mean,

Here I am, stationary, battling for position.

I have to make it to fifty! Again, this is a huge deal to an entry-level, low-drafted player like me. I get to the rink and I'm still being careful not to slice my finger on the blade of my skate or blowtorch myself in the face taking care of my sticks.

As the warm-up approaches I decide to wear a helmet. I never wear a helmet during warm-ups. But there is no way I'm risking getting a puck shot at my head or losing my edge and sliding into the boards headfirst. I get all bundled up and make sure I'm extra careful. I'm telling myself, "We got to get this game in the books. One shift. Just one shift." Naturally, the rest of my team knows how important this game is to me. The game starts and I get my shift. Game played. Number fifty. I do nothing on the shift. I'm just glad to get number fifty in the books. Once the shift ends I come down and high five the whole bench as if I have just scored the game winner in Maple Leaf Gardens. I made it. No matter what happens now, my salary is $140,000 for the rest of the season, and the next year it's $150,000, whether I'm in the AHL or NHL. To celebrate my one way deal, I take anybody who wants to come out to Rod Langway's bar and I pay for all the drinks.

Fast forward to the end of the season, and Capitals General Manager Dave Poile approaches my agent Gene McBurney and wants to upgrade the contract and add an additional year. Gene calls me and I am all fired up. I was happy to have just made $140,000. I couldn't believe I was making that much. I have no idea how much a lot of money is. I really don't. I look at some third and fourth line guys who are making $300-$400,000 a year and say, "Man, if I ever could get to $300,000 I would be the happiest guy in the world. I'd love to get Paul MacDermid money. That must be unbelievable!"

In my rookie season with the Caps, I played in 71 games, scored 12 goals, had 14 assists and was a +18 playing on the third line with Dale Hunter and Pat Elynuik. I also earned 124 penalty minutes. We were a pretty productive third line. Well, when the playoffs arrived our coach, Terry Murray, felt like he should go with a veteran guy and replaced me on the third line with Bobby Carpenter. Worse still, he basically decided to go with three lines while I wasted away on the fourth line. At that point, I thought Bobby Carpenter was just about done. And I told him! For fun, I made a $100 bet with Bobby that I would outlast him in the NHL. I thought this was easy money, but Bobby went on to play six more years and I barely beat him out. You still owe me a hundred bucks, Bobby Carpenter.

So, Randy Burridge and I were relegated to the end of the bench as we opened up the 1993 Stanley Cup Playoffs against the New York Islanders. Randy scored 23 goals in 1991-92 before tearing his ACL and spent all of this season trying to get back. He played just four games during the 92-93 NHL season.

We won Game 1 against the Islanders, 3-1. Well, at this point, Randy and I were basically "grocery sticks." You know, those things at the grocery store that you use to keep your groceries separated from the person in front of you as you unload your cart? We were human grocery sticks, separated from the rest of the team. We would play a couple of shifts in the first period and then sit the rest of the game.

We were NHL doormen opening and closing the door on the bench all game long.

In Game 2, Randy and I had our couple of first period shifts and then sat the rest of the game. Well, Game 2 went into double overtime, so that was a lot of sitting. Also, before Game 2, I left a couple of tickets for a girl I met at a bar in Maryland called The Green Turtle. She brought her friend to the game and I could see them in the crowd as I was closing and opening the door. During one of my early shifts, I got into a scuffle with Islander defensemen Rich Pilon. We were along the boards and Pilon says, "Let's go!"

He was asking me for a fight.

"Take your visor off, you Russian puke," I respond.

He says, "No problem." And takes his whole helmet off.

I'm thinking, "Oh, boy."

I throw a couple of early rights and then he wallops me with four big lefts in a row and knocks my helmet across the rink. I can still see it sliding across the ice.

After I serve my time and return to the bench, Dale Hunter asks me what I was doing out there.

I say, "What do you mean?"

He says, "He's an Indian from the west!"

I say, "I thought he was a Russian!"

Well, I sat the rest of the game, opening the door, and chirping at Islander center Ray Ferraro all game long. Now, Ray was never one to back down from a verbal confrontation. NHL Productions should have put microphones on the both of us having our battle of wits. It's no wonder we are now both in the television business.

Finally, after watching three full periods in a row without playing, Randy and I jumped on the ice for another shift, and bam! Brian Mullen scored the overtime winner for the Islanders to even the series at one game each. And to really make matters worse, the girl I left the tickets for must have really been impressed with the public Pilon beating I took. She didn't wait for me after the game and bolted. I never saw her again.

The series shifted to Long Island. In Game 3, the same thing happened. It was hockey Groundhog Day with Stumpy and Jonesy. Randy Burridge and I played a couple of shifts in the first period and then sat the entire game. Like I said, Game 3 went to overtime. And after sitting since the first period, Burridge and I stepped on the ice for our first shift in about two hours, and bam! My buddy Ray Ferraro scored the overtime winner for the Islanders. Well, Ray gave it to me good as our teams left the ice. I think I was telling him he looked like PGA golfer Cory Pavin during the game and he was calling me his caddy. "Who's my caddy, Jonesy?!"

Game 4 arrived and once again Burridge and I played a couple of shifts in the first period and sat again all night long. Game 4 went to double overtime. After sitting since the first period, Randy and I finally got a shift in double overtime and before you know it, another goal! And it was farging Ray Ferraro again! I was skating off the ice thinking this can't be happening. Ferraro was at the beginning of an unbelievable postseason. He went on to score 13 goals in 18 Islander playoff games during the Playoffs.

The next day at practice, Terry Murray went up to Randy Burridge and told him he wasn't playing in the next game. I looked at Randy and said, "I told you I had my man."

We went on to lose to the Islanders in six games.

Well, my agent Gene called me after the playoffs and said the Capitals were offering a new three year deal that would pay me $270,000, $280,000, and $330,000. I remember during one of my strenuous workouts that summer, which in this case meant hanging out at my friend's pool in Brantford, saying, "This is amazing! That's almost a million dollars!" I was just so fired up about it. I couldn't believe the Caps were offering an extension.

My friends, of course were like, "Sign it! Sign it!"

So, I signed the deal. In year one, the 1993-1994 season, I scored sixteen goals in sixty-eight games, but didn't do much in the playoffs, just one assist in eleven games.

It was during that season that I was introduced to new coach, Jim Schoenfeld. We had gotten off to a slow start (it didn't help that Dale Hunter was sitting out his 20 game suspension for hitting Pierre Turgeon during the previous playoffs) and in the middle of the season Terry Murray was fired as head coach and replaced by Jim Schoenfeld. Schoenfeld was a good, solid, tough defenseman for thirteen NHL seasons. In 1979-80, he was a +60! After he retired he became a coach. First for the Sabres, then the Devils, and then for me and the Capitals.

Jim Schoenfeld and I butted heads from day one. He was a fitness nut and I was not. He was all business and I was not. It would be a rocky three years.

Like I said, the Capitals season was bumbling along and G.M. David Poile fired Terry Murray while the team was in Buffalo and replaced him with Jim Schoenfeld, who was in Buffalo doing mattress commercials on television at the time. Meanwhile, I was back in Washington rehabilitating an injured wrist with Enrico Ciccone and Jason Woolley when we heard the news about the coaching change. We knew Schoenfeld was a tough guy, but it was a fresh start and that's always a good thing.

Well, the team got back from the road trip and we started to practice with them again. After the first practice, Schoenfeld called me aside and said, "I hear you like to yap a lot."

"I guess so," I told him.

Schoenfeld then says, "We're going to have a little skate after practice for you guys who haven't been playing." So, right off the bat things weren't going smoothly, although I was more confused than turned off. Well, he skated us into the ground, and we all know how much I enjoy that.

After our "bag" skate was complete, Schoenfeld told me and Ciccone, "You can do this for the next ten days while we are on our upcoming road trip, or you can go down to the AHL and play six games with the Portland Pirates and do a conditioning stint."

Thinking I didn't want to skate like I just did for another ten days I said, "I'll gladly go to Portland!" So, I go down to Portland and score five goals and seven assists in six games and have way more fun than I would have had skating all day!

The season was going along when I got injured again and had to miss a couple more games. During this time, I go out to dinner with Dale Hunter, Craig Berube, and "Sluggo" our equipment guy. The team had lost the last couple of games and I told the guys at dinner that they were going to get skated hard the next day. I say, "I'm like a church mouse, boys. I'm just keeping to myself, not causing any problems and I'll be laughing while you boys get bag skated tomorrow!

I'm not saying a word while you guys keep losing. I'm a church mouse. He can't get me! You guys are done. Schoney's gonna bury you guys tomorrow."

Frank Costello was the strength coach at the time, and at the next day of practice he was given a workout routine by Schoenfeld to have me follow. With the team losing, Schoney wanted everybody to pay a price, and rightly so. So, Frank starts reading this long, arduous list of about twenty exercises for me — the new church mouse in town — to do. After about the eighteenth item, I blurt out, "What is this guy, Frank, an asshole or something?"

Well, unbeknownst to me, Schoney was around the corner and behind Frank. He goes right up to Frank, not me, and tells him to come to his office. Schoney tells Frank to tell me to wait for him after practice when he will work me out himself. So, I'm sitting in the room while the rest of the guys are getting skated into the ground. All kinds of things are going through my mind and Frank is not helping me any by laughing his ass off at my situation.

So, Schoney, of course, gives me the workout from hell. I'm wearing a weight vest, I'm lifting, lifting, lifting, I'm sweating like I've never sweated before. Meanwhile, the rest of the team is showered and walking to their cars to go home. Unfortunately for me, they have to walk by the gym. Well, I've never seen anyone laugh harder than those guys who were watching me get just buried into the ground. Especially the guys who were out with me at dinner the night before, when I claimed I was just a church mouse not causing any problems. Dale Hunter screamed, "I'm a church mouse!!," as he walked by the room and into the parking lot. That was the first of my many battles with Jim Schoenfeld.

The next year, 1994-95, was the lockout year. No hockey or no money until January. After the lockout, the NHL did what they could to keep us out of the playoffs by scheduling 12 of our first 19 games on the road. We won just four of them. But we finished strong and made the playoffs. I scored 14 goals in the 40 regular season games, which projects to about 30 goals over a regular length 82 game season. My 14 goals were second to Peter Bondra's 34 that season.

We played the Penguins in the playoffs and were up three games to one in the best of seven series, but lost the last three games 6-5, 7-1, and 3-0, to lose in seven games. I had a productive series against the Penguins, scoring four goals and making four assists for eight points in seven games.

I was about to enter the last year of my three year contract, which meant that my salary was going to go from $280,000 to $330,000. A nice $50,000 raise that you could really see in the ol' paycheck. You don't really notice a ten thousand dollar raise spread out over the course of a season. But, 50K more, and you're thinking HBO. You would think, given how happy that $140,000 made me just a few short years ago, that $330,000 would make me completely content. I mean, I made the mountaintop. I was going to make Paul MacDermid money! However, the Capitals had Rob Pearson, and he was due to make $500,000 that season.

Rob was a big time Junior player in the OHL for the Belleville Bulls and the Oshawa Generals. He was a first round pick for the Maple Leafs in 1989, twelfth overall. He scored 57 goals for Oshawa and finished his Junior career with sixteen goals in sixteen OHL play-off games. However, he scored just 49 goals in 192 games as a Leaf and they traded him to Washington for Mike Ridley.

Mike had been a solid player for the Capitals and was at the end of his career. He played the lockout year in Toronto and finished his career in Vancouver. Ridley played 866 NHL games and scored 292 goals. A real workman-like two way player. The kind of guy who never said a word on the ice. Nothing fancy, nothing extraordinary. Just a good player. He played college hockey in Canada so I could identify with the late bloomer in him.

Now, Rob Pearson is a great guy and it has nothing to do with him personally, but he had played thirty-two games during the lockout season for us and didn't score a goal. No goals and six assists as a winger. He did score a game-winning goal for us in the playoffs against the Penguins, but that no goal total in the regular season was driving me crazy. I mean, I was second on the team in goal scoring the year before, Rob had none, and he was set to make $500,00 to my $330,000. I couldn't stomach it. It was my introduction to the financial game of the NHL.

That being said, I had no idea how the negotiating game worked. I called my agent and asked him what was going on? I got so upset at what I perceived as a "lazy" attitude that I told him, "You're fired."

He says, "What do you mean?"

I reply, "You're fired. I'm doing the contract myself. I'm doing it myself." I think Gene found it more amusing than anything. He wasn't making much of a commission off of me.

I called Capitals G.M. David Poile and told him that I had fired my agent and wanted to meet with him to talk about my contract even though I still had a year left on my current deal.

He says, "Ahhh, sure. I'll meet with you." I'm sure he was licking his chops at the chance to negotiate with a knob like me. He was probably saying, "Look at this pigeon!"

There was a day set up that summer when the Capitals were going to unveil their new uniforms at Planet Hollywood. Personally, I didn't think they should change the old Capitals jerseys. I'd still like to see them go back to the original red, white, and blues. Anyway, me and Dale Hunter and some of our teammates, went to this new uniform unveiling. I saw David Poile at the ceremony and asked him when we could we meet. He says, "Tomorrow."

The next day I show up at Poile's office for my big contract meeting wearing shorts and a tee shirt, carrying a briefcase.

Oh, by the way, the briefcase is empty.

I walk into Poile's office and sit down with my empty briefcase.

We start talking and Poile is curious as to what I am looking for.

I'm entering the last year of my deal and set to make $330,000. I look him in the eye and say, "David. If I have to make less money than Rob Pearson this year I'm going to retire."

Remember, Pearson is set to make $500,000 after scoring no goals in the regular season, while I was set to earn $330,000 after being second on the team in goals. I say, "I'm going to retire. And I mean it."

He says, "What?"

I reply, "I will not take less money than Rob Pearson. I can't stomach that. It's not going to happen. I'm not going to make less than Rob Pearson this year."

Poile says, "I see. Well, this is the tough part of negotiations. This is where having an agent would be a little helpful for you. The agent serves as a buffer. I have to tell you what you do wrong, what you do poorly, and what you need to improve on."

I say, "David, don't worry about it. I'm Keith Jones the agent, Keith Jones the player is waiting outside the door."

Poile then has one of his lieutenants, Todd Warren, a guy we called Scoop, gather some comparable statistics of other players around the NHL. He brings the list in and Poile compares me to guys like Tom Fitzgerald, Travis Green, and Bill Lindsay. And I'm like, "I've never even heard of these guys. They got nothin'."

Then, as I had been doing from time to time throughout our meeting, I open up my briefcase and peer inside, just for effect. Remember, it's empty. I look in like I'm breaking down my own numbers, close the briefcase, and then continue.

Poile says, "Look at Mikael Renberg. He just scored 26 goals and had 57 points in 47 games for the Flyers. Look at the goal scoring he's done and you want to make as much as him?"

I say, "David. If I played with Eric Lindros and John LeClair, I would have more points than Mikael Renberg. I believe that."

And I did believe that. I was slowly figuring out the NHL. I was getting more comfortable and beginning to understand what to do and how to play to get the most out of my strengths. I was getting confident. Strangely, a few years later I would end up playing with Lindros and LeClair.

At the end of my meeting with Poile, I reiterated that I wanted $500,000 and wouldn't play for less. He said we would talk again and that was it. About a week later I get a call from my teammate Dave Poulin, who hears I'm acting as my own agent and negotiating my own deal. He says there is no way I'm doing this by myself. Poulin tells me that Steve Mountain was his agent, and that he would take over as mine. He basically drafts Mountain for me. I never really had a say in it. I'm like, whatever, Poulin is smarter than me! So, I head home to Brantford not really knowing what will happen. Two weeks later I get a call from Steve Mountain. He says, "You're all set. You'll make $500,000 this season." Just like that.

The meeting with Poile was just one of those things where I wanted to find out what I could do. It was part of that new-found courage and perspective I had gained a few years earlier during our family tragedy.

Like a lot of things in my life, I look back now and say, "What was I thinking?" But, who knows? Maybe I convinced Poile I deserved to make $500,000 that day. Maybe the briefcase and the confidence and the unconventionality of the moment made an impression. If I had said nothing and just played out the last year of my deal, I would have made $170,000 less.

It's an instance where speaking up paid off. Either way, I was happy. Rob Pearson wasn't making more money than me. And I was making more than Paul MacDermid.

That being said, I really started to hit my stride in terms of understanding my role as a yapper and a pest, during my fourth year in the NHL. That season, 1995-96, I was scoring goals and was a plus player, so that gave me the freedom to take some chances to really up the ante emotionally. I was beginning to get a feel for the game, and that included taking penalties early in games, especially playoff games, to set a tone and to test the other team. It would serve me very well later in my career, when I played for the Flyers in the 2000 Stanley Cup Playoffs. It didn't go as well in 1996.

As the 1996 Stanley Cup Playoffs approached I had twenty four career playoff games under my belt. However, I ended the season with a torn groin injury, a scoring drought, and more battles with my coach, Jim Schoenfeld. My last goal was over two months ago. On February 8 in Calgary, I scored my eighteenth goal of the season. It would be my last.

The '96 playoffs began, and our opponents were the Pittsburgh Penguins. My pal Craig Berube and I were on the sidelines with injuries. We won the first two games in Pittsburgh, and then the series shifted to Washington and the Penguins came back to win Game 3, 4-1. Then they won Game 4, on Petr Nedved's goal with 44 seconds left in the fourth overtime, 3-2. Jaromir Jagr and Sergei Zubov assisted. The series was tied two games each.

The series shifts back to Pittsburgh for Game 5. The day before at practice, Schoenfeld says, "Jonesy, you're in, and so are you Berube. You're playing." So, with one practice under our belt, the Chief and I are playing against the Penguins. We lose Game 5, 4-1. I play a good amount, but don't accomplish much my first game back from the groin injury. We're now down three games to two, and the series returns to Washington.

Schoenfeld starts me in Game 6. I'm really fired up. The season ended poorly and I'm looking to make up for it in this game. During my first shift of Game 6, the puck goes behind the Pittsburgh net and Ken Wregget goes to play it. And I run him. Penguins defenseman J.J. Daigneault jumps me and we start fighting. I get two minutes for running Wregget and a five minute major penalty for fighting Daigneault.

As I go to the box, I'm praying the Penguins power play doesn't score. Sure enough they do. After the period we head to the dressing room, down 2-0. We're all curious how Schoney's going to react, especially me.

Schoney heads to the board and starts going through what he wants us to do. When he's finished, he looks at me and says, "Jonesy, you owe us a goal!" I look at him and kind of nod my head. Then he says, "No! That's not right. You owe us two goals for taking that stupid penalty to start the game!" and then walks out of the room. Once he's gone, I look over at Berube and Dale Hunter and say, "Isn't that kind of pushing it a little bit? I haven't scored in over two months! Don't hold your breath!"

We went on to lose 3-2, and my fourth season in the NHL was over.

#26 Keith Jones   Right Wing

I was at my best when I wasn't moving, seen here during my rookie season.

CHAPTER 8
"I TOLD YOU BOYS YOU'D MISS ME"

As I began my fifth year with the Washington Capitals, I was making $750,000. The season before I had a career-high 18 goals and 23 assists in 68 games. But the 1996-97 season was not starting off well. In the second game of the season, I took a left hook sucker-punch from Bill Huard of the Stars, and spent the night in the hospital getting checked out. Looking back, I'm sure I had a concussion. I had all the symptoms: fogginess, headaches, and general lethargy. The lethargy part was actually pretty normal for me, but the other symptoms told me something was wrong.

I continued playing because that's what you did back then. You don't know what exactly is wrong, you just assume you're in a slump and try to get out of it through sheer determination. So many slumps were endured in those days by guys who had concussions and weren't feeling right, but didn't know what the problem was. Everyone just figured effort was the cure.

I had a very bad couple of weeks at the start of the season, and I was really lethargic in practice. Off the ice, I was tired and sleeping all the time like I was back in college. I'm talking sixteen, seventeen hours a night. And I'm not a sleeper. At the same time I had to get through those demanding Jim Schoenfeld practices.

One day, after a long, hard practice that ended with bag skating, I laid down on the ice and started doing snow angels. I was just beat, laying there on the ice counting the lights at the top of the arena and making snow angels. While I'm performing this world-class-athlete movement, Schoenfeld skates over, peers down, and says, "What in the hell is wrong with you now?"

I look up at him and say, "I don't feel well. I'm exhausted."

He replies, "That's it! You're going to the Mayo Clinic." The Mayo Clinic turns out to be the local doctor's office, down the street about a block away. I go there to get some blood work done and now my mind is racing. I'm thinking cancer, leprosy, polio, or any other number of other horrible diseases. It doesn't ever occur to me that it might be a concussion from that Huard punch, even though I have classic concussion symptoms. My mind can overwork that way sometimes.

So, I go and have the blood work done and wait for the results. In the meantime, we play a couple more games and I'm still not playing very well, but I'm afraid to ask anybody about the blood work. Now the stress of not knowing the results from the blood tests are compounding with my lethargy to produce one inept NHL player. Meanwhile, we're off to a 5-6 start. I have two goals and three assists in the eleven games.

I go back to the Marriott across from the Islanders' arena, have a bite to eat, and head up to bed at 7:00 p.m. I fall asleep again and sleep until 9:00 a.m. the next morning. Fourteen hours in all and I'm still tired.

I head over to the practice rink and finally ask our trainer, Stan Wong, about the results of my blood work. He says they should be in at any time, and maybe even in time for the game against the Islanders that night. I go out and feel a little better during the morning skate because I had slept so much the night before.

Now, since it is a one-day road trip, I perform my customary one-day road trip packing routine. My packing routine consists of wearing my one suit and putting a toothbrush in the inside pocket. That is it. No suitcase, no change of clothes, no moisturizer, no nothing. I change my underwear with the laundry from the arena. I take the team's underwear home after we skate and switch them with my skivvies so I'm not that dirty. I wear the same cheap suit, tie and jacket from the Barney Miller collection.

After my afternoon nap, I wear my Abe Vigoda-endorsed suit over to Nassau County Coliseum for the game against the Islanders. I ask Stan Wong about the blood work again and he says it should be in any time now. I go about my business and begin to get ready for the warm up. I'm sitting next to Dale Hunter in the locker room and we're doing the usual, shooting the breeze and getting ready for the game.

As we're getting ready, the blood work and my health are still on my mind. I continue getting dressed while Dale Hunter and I chat. I finish putting my first skate on. At that moment Jim Schoenfeld comes into the room. Schoney is a big, intimidating man and he never comes into the locker room before warm ups. Of course, he comes over right to me. Him looking down, me looking up. Me about to put my other skate on while waiting for Schoney's other shoe to drop. Now what?

Schoney looks down at me with a concerned look on his face and says, "Jonesy, I need to see you in my office right now."

I look over at Dale Hunter and all I'm thinking is that they got the results from the blood work. It's been the only thing on my mind for weeks. I'm dying because the look on Schoney's face is straight from Doctor Death. He may as well be the Grim Reaper with a whistle. Immediately, I get that instant stomachache when you know something terrible has happened or is about to happen. I get up with one skate on and amble over to the coach's office to get my death card from the hands of Moby Dick.

With my one skate one, I "limp" into the tiny office that the Islanders provide for the visiting team's coach. I sit down, anticipating hearing the results of my blood work, which I have now presumed to be catastrophic. Jim Schoenfeld looks at me and says, "Son, I have some terrible news."

Now I know, I'm a goner with an incurable disease! The knot in my stomach is now the size of a grocery bag full of franks and beans. I mean I can't believe it. This is it! I really believe I'm about to receive my death sentence. I'm clearly in the beginning stages of a slow, painful, excruciating death. It's the only thought on my mind.

So, there I am, waiting for Schoney to fill in the blank regarding just which, precisely, incurable disease I have.

He reiterates. "Son, I have really bad news. This is really bad news."

And I'm like, "What?!"

Finally, he tells me. "You've been traded."

And I say, in a burst of uninhibited joy, "Thank God!"

Schoenfeld, of course, was shocked at my response, and said incredulously, "What?! You are taking this a lot better than I thought you would!"

At that point, I said something along the lines of, "You're a great guy away from the rink, but as a coach I can't stand you!" A really ignorant thing to say, looking back. But, I was so relieved that I wasn't dying.

Jim Schoenfeld probably doesn't know to this day that the real reason I was glad to hear I was being traded was that I wasn't receiving bad news about the blood work I had taken a week before.

What's funny is, I still didn't know what the results of the blood tests were, but I was so relieved, I started feeling better instantly!

So, I asked Schoney where I was being traded.

He says, "Colorado."

I say, "For who?" This was my first trade, so I was very curious of what my value was to another team, and the league in general.

He says, "I can't tell ya."

I say, "What do you mean you can't tell me?"

Schoney says, "We can't find one of the guys."

Come to find out, that guy was Chris Simon, and he was

holding out because of a contract dispute with the Avalanche. Simon was out bear hunting in the deep woods and they couldn't get in touch with him.

I went back into the room and said, "Hey, boys we'll see you in the finals!" They ask me what I am talking about and I say, "I've been traded to Colorado! This is awesome!" It was the weirdest feeling being traded because the Capitals were family to me. I loved the players, especially Dale Hunter, who calls me and everyone "Chum." I had been drafted by the Capitals in 1988, and they'd owned my rights until that day, November 2, 1996. It didn't hit me at the time though.

That being said, I was very excited to be going to Colorado because they had just won the Stanley Cup, not to mention the long haul with the Capitals and my daily battles with Schoenfeld. And, of course, I was glad I wasn't going to die. At least not then. Not on Long Island.

The Capitals went out and lost that night to the Islanders, 6-1. I made sure to call Dale Hunter the next day, and said to him, "I told you boys you'd miss me!"

CHAPTER 9

PLANES, TRAINS, AND AUTOMOBILES

Although I was no longer a rookie, I felt like one again after Jim Schoenfeld told me I'd been traded to Colorado. I was like, now what? What do I do? Where do I go? This was 1996 and cell phones were not yet the full-fledged necessity for human existence that they are now. I didn't have a cell and it was making life a little difficult during my quest to become a member of the Colorado Avalanche.

Our Capitals P.R. guy, Todd Warren, told me I'd have to call Avalanche G.M. Pierre Lacroix to find out where I was supposed to go and how this trade business was going to work. Again, I had no cell phone. All I had in my pocket were a couple of quarters. I grabbed my gear, my sticks and my toothbrush. Remember, I had nothing else in my possession but the cheap suit I was wearing and the toothbrush in my pocket due to my preference for traveling light. I'd have to go shopping when I landed. All my stuff was back in Washington. The only clothes I had, including underwear, were on my back and butt.

Meanwhile, my fiancé Laura was visiting her family in Michigan and I didn't even know how to reach her. She had moved down to Washington from Michigan to be with me and was just getting comfortable in her new Washington D.C. environment. Now I had to tell her she would have to move again. This time to Colorado.

With my hockey gear in tow, I needed to find a way to call Pierre Lacroix but I didn't know where to get a phone. I meandered through the concourse of the Nassau Coliseum, where all the Islander fans were milling about as the Islanders and Capitals went through their warm-up and prepared for the game.

There I was, Mr. NHL player. I had my hockey bag over my shoulder, six aluminum Easton sticks with an Andrew Brunette curve in my left hand, and a gnarly toothbrush in my inside pocket. I thought Andrew Brunette had the best curve in the NHL and was using his at the time.

Wandering through the concourse, I was like a lost child at Disneyworld. Except, instead of looking for my mommy, I was looking for a telephone. The people on the concourse must have thought I was some fanatical fan who had brought their gear to the game with the hope that Islander G.M. Mike Milbury would sign them up to play that night.

I finally found find a pay phone on the concourse and called Pierre Lacroix. He told me I had ninety minutes to get to New York's LaGuardia Airport to catch a cross country flight to Anaheim.

I was like a lost puppy in a jungle, having never been traded before. Lacroix told me to get a taxi, get to the airport, walk up to the counter, get on my flight, and I'd be on my way. I actually wrote those instructions down, and then headed outside the arena to hail a cab.

I flagged a cab and told the driver to take me to the airport, and hopped in the back after putting my gear in the trunk. My heart was racing over what had taken place so far that evening: I found out that, apparently I wasn't dying. I just got traded. I was on my way to Anaheim for the following night's game between the Ducks and my new team, the Avalanche. And this was all in about an hour. I was sitting there in the back of that cab saying to myself, "What in the hell just happened?"

I got to the airport and headed up to the counter to get my ticket. The lady behind the counter told me I'd be in economy class and I say, "No, no, no, there must be a mistake. I'm supposed to be in first class." I later got a bill from the Avalanche saying I owed them the difference between the economy and first-class ticket!

The flight had to go through Atlanta. I was enjoying my first-class ride and having a couple of libations as we landed in Georgia. Before my flight to Anaheim, I found another pay phone to call my fiancé, Laura, to tell her about the trade and the fact we would be moving to Colorado. I was able to track down her phone number in Michigan and call her. She answers the phone and I tell her I've been traded. Laura answers, "I know, I just saw it on the bottom line on ESPN 2." Remember, Jim Schoenfeld said he couldn't tell me who I was traded for because they couldn't reach one of the guys.

I say to Laura, "Who was I traded for?"

She says, "Chris Simon and Curtis Leschyshyn."

I reply, "Wow! Two guys who just helped them win a Stanley Cup. For me!" To get traded for two guys like that was good for my self-esteem. You never know your value in the NHL until someone pays a price to get you. The Capitals also sent a first-round pick to Colorado, which they would use to draft Scott Parker.

I got on my connecting flight and headed to Anaheim as the Capitals were losing 6-1 against the Islanders. Meanwhile, my new teammates were in Buffalo playing a scoreless tie against the Sabres. So, I actually arrived in Anaheim before they did and wouldn't meet them until the next morning.

After a night's sleep in an Anaheim hotel, I headed down to meet my teammates at the pregame meal. There was no morning skate because of the game in Buffalo the night before and the subsequent cross-country flight.

I walked into a room full of guys who had just lost two popular teammates that had helped them win a Stanley Cup the previous spring. It's always a rough walk for a professional athlete who is traded to a new team, especially in the NHL, where, culturally, the players are so much alike, and probably the closer for it. The fact that I was a hated player didn't help much either. I had played well against the Nordiques and then the Avalanche, and I was always on my worst behavior against them. Elbows, vile comments, you name it.

As it turns out, despite my history, things instantly went well with my new teammates. The 1996-97 edition of the Colorado Avalanche was a great group of guys with a winning attitude. Marc Crawford was the coach and he was just the best. I think he recognized some offensive potential in me back in those games where I played well. And he understood the pest factor I brought to a team, and appreciated my knowing when to stir it up, to wake up the team and get them going. It's a role with a fine line. You drive the other team crazy without driving your own teammates crazy.

Right away, at the Avalanche team meal, I picked up where I left off with my smartass message to Dale Hunter and the Capitals. I told Patrick Roy, Joe Sakic, Peter Forsberg, and all these great Avalanche players during out first meal together, "Don't worry boys, everything is good. Jonesy is here to save the day."

CHAPTER 10
ROCKY MOUNTAIN HIGH

My first game with the Avalanche didn't go so well. We were playing in Anaheim and leading 1-0 when I took a penalty late in the game. Jari Kurri took a dive, and I was in the box, when the Ducks tied the game at 19:58 of the third period on a goal by Roman Oksiuta. (Who, incidentally, was the guy the Rangers had once traded to Edmonton to get Kevin Lowe.)

Three nights later, however, things started to click for me in a big way with the Avs. I scored two goals and made an assist in a 4-1 win in San Jose, beating Kelly Hrudy twice and assisting on a Sakic empty netter.

Two nights later in Phoenix I scored the eventual game winner on a power play against Nikolai Khabibulin. Then to top it all off, I played my first game at home as a member of the Avalanche and scored, once again, the eventual game winner. That game was against the Montreal Canadiens, and my winning shot was on a power play against the legendary Pat Jablonski.

We hit the road again, winning on Long Island, where the whole trade odyssey began, and Detroit. I was now 5-1 with the Avs, and we were going 9-0-2. It was a good time to roll with the Avs. They were defending Stanley Cup champions, and were winning every night.

Good times. Good times.

It was difficult not to play well with this team. I was playing with Peter Forsberg and Valeri Kamensky because Claude Lemieux was injured. Forsberg was truly a once in a lifetime player. He made everyone who played with him better. He was unselfish and always opted to make the right play. I was a give-and-go guy who didn't want to carry the puck. If Peter passed me the puck, I passed it right back to him, and players like Peter like that. He was also physical, and he never got knocked off the puck. I was also the kind of guy who would go get loose pucks and give them to Peter. He was the master, I was the dog.

Off the ice, Forsberg was a real class act. He had a certain aura about him. He didn't come across like he knew he was great, but he was. He was a humble, modest superstar. A real comfortable person to be around.

Valeri Kemensky was a real talent who was also unselfish. He would deke out half of the other team and then slide it over to you for the empty netter. A real-great guy.

He, fellow Russian Alexi Gusarov, and Latvian Sandis Ozolinsh were all cigarette smokers. After a long flight we would see them down at the end of the ramp smoking their road flares with amazing enthusiasm.

Gusarov drove a big Hummer at the time. He used to pick me up to go to practice because we both lived way up in the mountains. When he drove up to my place, I could always see the little red light at the end of his cigarette, all lit up through the windshield. He was a real character. Adam Foote, his D-partner, was by far the most important defenseman on the team. Great guy with an unbelievable desire to do whatever was needed to win. He is still one of my best friends away from the game!

The team kept winning, and I was having the best year of my career. We were a fun and very close-knit team because they had just won the Cup. That builds a bond for life. But they still made me feel like I was a part of the team from the start. The whole attitude was, "We are going to win the Cup." That's why we were there and that's what they did.

In my mind, the Avalanche was Patrick Roy's team. Despite all the great names, Patrick Roy was the dominant presence. He was the only goalie I never considered shooting high on during practice.

Patrick was so important that you didn't want to hurt him. When he came up to you after a game and said, "you just had a good game," you did. He wasn't going to tell you that you played well unless you did. It was always open and honest. The ultimate leader.

It didn't matter who you were. It didn't matter if you were Joe Sakic, Peter Forsberg, or Adam Foote. If Patrick Roy felt that you needed to give the team more, he told you. Patrick demanded the best out of everyone and himself. He didn't waste words. He didn't speak just so coaches or the media would hear him. He spoke with the sole purpose of making the team better. He always timed his words well.

He will be an impact guy in the NHL again as either a General Manager or a coach because of his personality and because he knows the game so well. He was the guy who would fix the penalty kill if there was a problem. He would watch the video and make the adjustments. An unbelievable competitor. He remains the most impressive figure I encountered during my NHL career, and the greatest leader I've ever played with.

I am keeping my on the puck, attempting to beat Chris Osgood.

After Claude Lemiuex returned, he went back on the Forsberg-Kamensky line. I then had to slum with Joe Sakic and Adam Dead-marsh. Joe Sakic was a tremendous leader by example. He did everything right — off-ice training, practice, and his consistent play during the games — the complete package. Joe wore the C as captain, but he let other guys share in the leadership role. Some guys monopolized the power in the room. Joe shared the responsibility. It was never about Joe. It was about the team, and that's a big reason why the Avalanche had been so successful for so long.

With all of that Hall of Fame talent around me, it wasn't difficult to understand why I was having the best year of my NHL career. The team was talented, driven, and focused. The culture of excellence was something so strong, it elevated everyone's game. Patrick Roy was on his way to a then-career-high 38 wins. Adam Deadmarsh scored a career-high 33 goals to lead the Avs that year.

Like I said, I was having the best year of my NHL career, eventually scoring more goals than Joe Sakic. I tied for fourth place on the team in scoring that season, with 23 goals in 67 games. We went on to win the Presidents Trophy, and our 49 wins remain the second most in Avalanche history, as do our 107 points. The only year better than this in Colorado history is the magical season of 2000-01, when Ray Bourque got to lift the Cup for the first and only time. That '00-01 Avs team had three more wins, eight fewer losses, and eleven more points than our '96-97 squad.

I was also having a lot of success on the power play. When I was traded to Colorado earlier that season, I had 12 career power play goals. In the 67 games I played with the Avs in '96-'97 I scored 13 power play goals, which was among the league leaders. I was playing on the second power play unit with Mike Ricci and Scott Young, while the other two spots were usually overlapping power play players like Joe Sakic and Sandis Ozolinsh.

Our coach, Marc Crawford, knew how to use everybody on the

team, and that's one of the reasons I respected him so much. We had a lot of superstars on that team, yet "Crow" kept everybody involved. He considered me a big part of the team, and that filled me with a confidence I had never felt before as an NHL player. Another thing I'll always admire about Marc Crawford is his ability to put out fires right away.

Here's an example. After scoring those three consecutive game winning goals right after my trade, I'm feeling great. Obviously I'm confident, flying around the ice, having never felt better about myself. I'm hearing only positive remarks from Marc because I'm playing so well. In my first six games with the Avs, we're 5-0-1 and I have three game winners. What's not to like?!

Well, game seven is in Buffalo, and we're playing the Sabres. We are down by one with about a minute and a half to go and we're trying to get the tying goal. Well, I'm feeling good and I can really feel this tying goal coming from my stick. The puck had been going in for me at the right time, and when you are on a team and you feel you are the best option, you might stay on the ice a little longer at the end of your shift. Especially if it's at a critical point in the game.

So, the clock continues to wind down in, and I'm feeling great. I have energy and really believe I am going to tie this game. After the tie in Anaheim in my Av debut, I have at least a point in every game. I haven't had one yet in Buffalo yet this night so I feel due.

Well, my extra-long shift does not result in the tying goal. The Sabres win, 5-4, and I experience my first loss as a member of the Avalanche.

We walk into the dressing room and it is naturally a little quiet after a loss. Well, I'm sitting there, dwelling on the fact that this is my first loss with the defending champions, when in comes Crawford. And then - Boom - like that he just buries me in front of the team. "Who in the f*** do you think you are?!" he screams in my face, "staying on the ice when we have Kemensky and Deadmarch waiting to get on!

That doesn't f★★★ing happen here."

Let me tell you, I was shocked. But he was right. And from that point on, it didn't matter who you were or how well you were playing. If it didn't fit in to what the team was doing, Crawford was going to let you know about it. Even if you were Peter Forsberg. And I respected Marc for that.

Meanwhile, I also realized that I was just one part of the Avalanche team. As well as I was playing, or thought I was playing, there were a lot of guys who were better than me, and Crawford wasn't the type to ever let you forget it. It was a great lesson.

That wasn't the only great thing that happened that year. Going into the season, I was having some groin problems. The Avalanche had a physical therapist named Fred Stoot who was a back/groin specialist. It turns out a lot of groin problems start with back issues, and Fred's pre-game adjustments kept my axles aligned, which did wonders for my groin. I had missed games because of groin problems earlier in my NHL career, but Fred made them a thing of the past. I felt fantastic the entire season and had tons of energy. I was on a great team, with a great organization, and playing with Hall of Fame players. I had never felt better.

By the time March rolled around, we were 46-19-9. I could feel that the Avs were going to repeat. How could life get any better? I was having a career year, I knew my salary would only keep rising, and I was going to be drinking champagne from the Stanley Cup in less than three months.

How could we lose? I figured we'd win the Cup, I'd get my name engraved on Lord Stanley forever, I'd bring it back to Brantford, Ontario, and raise a toast to all the Junior C players in Ontario past, present, and future. Yes, it was all good.

I was twenty-eight years old and at the top of my game.

CHAPTER 11
THE BEST OF TIMES, THE WORST OF TIMES

My 1996-97 dream season continued as we rolled into the shopping mall in Hartford and beat the soon-to-be Carolina Hurricanes 4-0 on March 25. In 1997, The Hartford Civic Center was actually enclosed within a shopping mall. You could buy a greeting card, a Whaler sweatshirt, a nasal decongestant, a pair of jeans, an Orange Julius, and check out a Whaler game, all in one trip. Today, the stores have been replaced by condominiums, and the Whalers replaced by the AHL Hartford Wolf Pack. 1996-97 was the final season of NHL hockey in Hartford. The organization would move to North Carolina over the summer.

The Whalers had 46 shots on goal that night, but Patrick Roy stopped them all for his seventh and final shutout of the season. We had just been shut out the game before by a strong Flyers team that eventually won the Eastern Conference, so it was good to get right back on the winning track with a shutout of our own. Everything was in line for a special spring and a confident march to Colorado's second straight Cup.

That all changed the next night in Detroit.

The Red Wings/Avalanche games had become the most heated rivalry in the NHL, and maybe all of North American sports, because of the star power, the excellence of the two teams, and maybe what had happened the previous spring.

Claude Lemieux's NHL career will be remembered for Conn Smythe Awards, Stanley Cup rings, and a mean streak that made him one of the NHL's most hated opponents, along the lines of

Ulf Samuelson. I definitely have a healthy respect for a guy who was the ultimate pest. He could score big goals and play well in the big games.

During the previous spring, when I was still with the Capitals, the Avalanches played the Red Wings in the Western Conference Finals. At 14:07 into the first period of Game 6 of the series, Lemieux checked Kris Draper from behind as Draper was along the boards near center ice. Draper's face crashed into the dasher, leaving him with a fractured upper jaw, a fractured cheekbone, a broken nose, a thirty-stitch cut inside his mouth, and five displaced teeth. Lemieux received a major penalty and a game misconduct for the hit, but Colorado went on to win the game 4-1 and the series 4-2. The Avs then went on to sweep the Florida Panthers in the Stanley Cup Final.

Draper said Lemieux never gave him a chance to protect himself, adding that it wasn't surprising, "because that's the kind of player he is and we all know that."

Lemieux says that it was is a clean shoulder-to-shoulder hit, and that the injury was an accident. He then goes on to say things like, "Who is Kris Draper?" which probably made the situation worse.

I think, if Lemieux had to do it all over again, he would have handled it differently in the media. He was suspended for the first two games of the 1996 Stanley Cup Final because of the hit, and the Wings vowed to get their revenge on him the following season. The Avalanche-Red Wing rivalry was born.

The best thing to come out of the Lemiuex-Draper incident, besides future passionate games, was Dino Ciccarelli's Hall of Fame quote after the game. Claude was tossed from the game after the Draper hit, but came out for the post series handshake in a Western Conference champion tee shirt and hat.

In the Red Wing locker room after the handshake, Ciccarelli tells the media, "I can't believe I shook his freakin' hand."

Fast-forward to March 26, 1997. It was a big ESPN game and Joe Louis Arena was packed as usual. We had shown our edge over the Red Wings the whole season, winning all three games, 4-1, 4-3, and 4-2. Three for three.

In our fourth and final regular season matchup, we got off to a fast start, with Valeri Kamensky scoring the only goal of the first period to make it 1-0.

Now, Claude Lemieux had missed the first half of the season with a torn abdominal muscle, an injury he received when his skate got caught in a rut on the ice during our October 5 game in Dallas. He didn't return until January 4, and therefore missed the first two games against Detroit of the season. The third game of the season against Detroit was in Colorado, just ten days before the big, nationally televised ESPN game. As I said, we had won that one 4-2. I scored a power-play goal 5:33 into the third period to break a 2-2 tie as we clinched our second straight Pacific Division title. Lemieux suited up for that game, his first against Detroit since the Draper incident, but nothing major happened in terms of revenge. Scotty Bowman told his boys to wait.

The wait was over that night in Detroit.

The police security Lemieux had at the hotel and on the way to the game was heavy. He was is a little worried about his safety in Detroit, as anybody would have been.

With us leading 1-0, all hell breaks loose with just under two minutes left in the first period. It begins with, of all players, Peter Forsberg and Igor Larianov wrestling at 18:22 of the first period. Darren McCarty uses this opportunity to jump Lemieux. Claude turtles. Now, McCarty should have been tossed from the game at this point, and linesman Ray Scampinello is trying to tell the young referee, Paul Devorski, that McCarty should be gone for instigating the fight. This was when the NHL still used the one referee system, and in situations like this, there is no way one man can see everything. Anyway, despite Scampinello's plea, Devorski keeps McCarty in the game and, in fact, merely gives him a double minor roughing penalty.

Lemieux is bloodied and battered, and has to be helped into the locker room to get himself together. Peter Forsberg leaves the game and doesn't return.

Patrick Roy then races to center ice to help Lemieux. That's Patrick. He's intercepted by Brendan Shanahan in a wild collision. Red Wing goalie Mike Vernon and our defenseman Adam Foote then join in. Once Patrick sees another goalie he squares off with Vernon. They exchange blows but, as the tape shows, Vernon lands a good shot on Patrick that buckles his knees for a second before the two resume exchanging blows. Vernon also draws a little blood from Patrick's face.

The incident really energizes the Red Wings in the second period. They outshoot us 23-7. However, Patrick is standing on his head and we score three goals on seven shots and lead after two 4-3. We take a 5-3 lead at 1:11 of the third as Kemensky completes a hat trick. It looks like we will sweep the season series despite the brawl.

But, fueled by the fight, the Red Wings keep coming with their energetic play and score two goals in the third period to tie the game 5-5. They outshoot us in regulation 46-19. The melee and the other fourteen fighting majors in the game really fire up Detroit. They take that into overtime and win on the first shot of OT by, guess who? Yep, Darren McCarty. The guy who jumped Claude Lemieux and then made him turtle.

A number of post game quotes reflect the intensity of the game.

> They're just a bunch of homers. They wanted
> to get back at Claude. My question is, why not at
> McNichols? I didn't see Draper out there. He had
> all the big guys fighting for him. But that's OK.
> I just want to know why they didn't do it at
> McNichols, why they waited six months.
>   — Mike Keane

By the way, I mentioned earlier that Patrick Roy was the best leader I ever played with. Well, Mike Keane was a close second. Complete package. Played a huge role in Cups win against Dallas.

> Guys just got paired off. I guess it was just God's will I got paired off with Lemieux. Forsberg started the whole thing. But that's the way hockey is. Sometimes things like that happen when you're seven years old and you have to wait until you're ten to get back at the guy. Some guys are still getting even for things that happened when they were kids. You just wait for your chances. It was intense.
> — Darren McCarty

> They should've had a few different calls. The ref [Paul Devorski] told me before the second period that he blew it. That's small consolation. The linesmen [Ray Scampinello] even said it should've been a gross misconduct on McCarty. It's a little ironic that he got the overtime goal ... We just didn't have quite enough to fend them off at the end. — Marc Crawford

> This is a game that brought the Red Wings together. Whether it was the first-period fighting or the overtime goal, a game like this only helps give you confidence to go into the playoffs. When you go to the playoffs, everybody has to be ready to do the job and stay together. Tonight showed the guys were willing to pay the price. — Mike Vernon

As I look back on the whole thing, I consider at it a testament to the genius of Scotty Bowman. The timing was never better to turn the tide of the Red Wing's season and ours. Bowman knew when to strike. At home and on a nationally televised ESPN game. It worked because that was the night our season turned for the worse.

Counting the Red Wing game, our record for the final eight games of the '96-97 regular season was 3-5. And while it was a lift to Detroit's psyche and perhaps a blow to ours, it was the injuries we received during the fights that really hurt us. Patrick Roy injured his shoulder in the melee and wasn't the same the rest of the year. Uwe Krupp hurt his back. Peter Forsberg got nicked. We didn't have a fighting team. Brett Severyn was all we really had.

Remember, Chris Simon was traded for me earlier in the season, and this is one night the Avs probably would have liked to have had Chris Simon's fists. Colorado lost that element in the trade for me, and Scotty Bowman exploited it.

Detroit always had tough teams. In my mind, Darren McCarty's goal in overtime against us won the Detroit Red Wings the Stanley Cup that year.

Despite the loss to Detroit, we still went on to win the Western Conference and the President's Trophy, and we were the number one seed as the 1997 Stanley Cup playoffs began.

Our opening round series was against the Blackhawks, who weren't a match for our team. Chicago had Tony Amonte, Chris Chelios, and Alexi Zhamnov, but beyond that, they didn't have the depth for us to consider them a serious threat.

In the Chicago playoff series I played on a line with Joe Sakic and Claude Lemieux. I mean, it's hard not to produce playing with those two guys. Sakic is definitely going to the Hall of Fame three years after he retires, and over time, Lemieux has a chance at enshrinement.

Chicago ends up giving us a tough series after we handily won Game 1 6-0. We win Game 2 3-1, but Chicago returned home, took care of business on home ice, and evened the series at two. We came out and blasted them in Game 5, 7-0, to take the series lead, three games to two.

I was playing very well in the series. I had three goals and three assists in the first five games. I was being my usual pest all over the ice as well, getting everybody on the Blackhawks going with my verbal barrage. I was once again the most hated man in town.

In Game 6 came the moment that would, from that point on, define my career, and in some ways, my life.

We were in the Chicago zone and working on offense. I got free on top of the circle and wired a shot that hit the cross bar and deflected high in the air. I crashed the net as the puck fluttered toward the ice.

When a situation like this occurs, you try to fight for position, while at the same time looking for the puck somewhere on the ice. Well, 6´6˝ 230-pound Eric Daze was in front of me and I had to try to eliminate this big donkey while trying to win the battle for the puck.

I went to kick Daze's legs out from underneath him, which was kind of a dirty play on my part. As I was doing it, I got the heel of my skate blade caught on the back of Daze's knee. The skate blade kind of snagged on his sock. Daze then fell, as my blade and my foot were stuck underneath his knee. All of Daze's 230 pounds fell on my knee. I heard a loud, distinct, POP! and immediately thought to myself, "That did not sound good." The strange thing was, despite the pop, it didn't hurt. It didn't hurt at all. It was the weirdest feeling because I knew it couldn't be good, but there was no pain.

I got up, and as I skated past the Blackhawks bench, they all gave it to me real good. They couldn't wait for me to get injured because of all the trash talking and standup material I was using on the ice. "Hey, Eric. Why the long face?"

I was probably asking for the injury the whole series, the way I was conducting myself. I got to the bench, headed into the locker room, and started walking around. I remember saying to myself, and the Avalanche trainers, "I think I'm all right."

Meanwhile, we ended up on a power play. Eric Daze was given a penalty for holding me on the play because he had held my leg between his. It put me in a vulnerable position, yes, but I started the whole cluster.

So, after convincing myself and the trainers that I thought I might be OK, I went back on the ice for the power play. Chicago ended up scoring a shorthanded goal. In the meantime, I couldn't feel my ankle. I didn't know where my leg was. It was the worst feeling I'd ever had in my hockey career. Legs are everything in most sports, and I couldn't feel one of mine. It was an awful feeling physically and emotionally, knowing that I was that injured, and what it might mean.

I knew we had a chance to win the Stanley Cup, and that I was a real important part of reaching that goal. I was at the point in my career where I felt I was going to go from an 18 to 20-goal guy to a 30-goal guy. I had enough respect from the Colorado coaching staff to be out there on the ice in key situations. You had to earn that important ice time, and I had. I had probably given coaches too many reasons not to trust me with more responsibility in the past. I hadn't been the greatest practice player in the world, and I joked around too much. And no matter what you bring to the big stage and the game, some coaches can't get past that initial impression you make on them.

I had a coach who understood who I was. Marc Crawford would come to me before a game or during the national anthem and say, "I want you to go after that guy tonight" or "Stir it up!" And I would. And I would be rewarded with power-play time and ice time with good players. There was a balance there that Marc Crawford recognized. Later in Philadelphia, Roger Neilson would recognize the same thing.

So, at the end of the first period in Chicago, I limped back to the trainer's room and sat on the trainer's table. The doctor came in and did the adjustment to see what condition my knee was in.

I had never injured my knee before, so this was all new to me. I didn't know my ACL from my MCL to the NFL back then. Now I know that when you twist your knee or fall on it, you can tear a stabilizing ligament, called the anterior cruciate ligament, that connects your thighbone to your shinbone. The anterior cruciate ligament, or ACL, unravels like a braided rope when it's torn and does not heal on its own. Anyway, as you may have guessed by now, the doctor looked at me and said, "I think you tore your ACL."

"What's that mean?" I asked.

He says, "It's not good. Not good. We'll have to have an MRI tomorrow and if it's your ACL you're looking at six to ten months of recovery time, if you can recover."

I say, "Really?"

Tears start to skate down my face as I think about everything this means for me and my NHL career. I am in a highly emotional state anyway from the intensity of playoff hockey. It's my first time on a legitimate Stanley Cup-contending team. And now this happens.

Marc Crawford comes in the room and tells me how badly he feels. I knew part of him had put me in the past already, because that's just the way it is. You have to move on. The rest of the team is not going to sit around and pat you on the back all night long. They have a job to do.

That night they completed the job. My teammates came back and won Game 6 against the Blackhawks to advance in the Western Conference playoffs. Their next opponent was the Edmonton Oilers.

On the bus ride back to the Chicago airport, I had a lot on my mind. My wife Laura had gone to the doctor that morning and found out she was pregnant with our daughter. She had cut out some pictures of me, her, a picture of a baby in a magazine, and letters from the magazine to spell out a new arrival was on the way. This was already a big day when the sun came up. Everything was going so well. I was starting a family and my NHL career was blossoming right before my eyes.

The day ended with me thinking about my knee and my hockey future. It was a difficult phone call home as I told Laura what had happened to my knee. My contract was ending, like, that day, and there I was with a serious knee injury.

If there was ever a time to get down on my knees, or knee, and pray, that was it.

CHAPTER 12

ON THE ROAD TO NOWHERE

I got back to Denver and it was MRI time. The MRI confirmed the severity of my knee injury, and it became time to talk about the different choices I had for ACL surgery. Everyone's knee structure is different, and what might work for one person might be the wrong choice for another.

I also decided to get a second opinion. The Avalanche was not happy about the whole second opinion business.

NHL teams like to do things with their own doctors, because in many cases doctors pay a fee to be called "The Official Doctor of The Colorado Avalanche." It's part of the business. There is a lot of pressure from players to stay in-house for business reasons.

So, I went and got a second opinion from Dr. Richard Stedman. Stedman had pioneered a successful program in sports trauma and reconstruction at The Tahoe Fracture and Orthopedic Medical Clinic before moving to Vail, Colorado, to open a clinic there. He has a great reputation working with the U.S. Ski Team and other well known athletes.

After looking at my MRI, Dr. Stedman said, "You know, this is going to be a very delicate surgery because you are so bowlegged." He warned me that it would be a very difficult surgery because of the structure of my knee. But he was confident he'd be able to find something that would do the trick, and my knee would be fine.

I went back to Denver and the Avalanche discovered that I had sought a second opinion. They were not happy. The Avalanche then began to put a lot of pressure on me to have their doctor perform the surgery. Now, remember, I didn't have a contract. My latest contract had just ended at the close of the 1996-97 season. At twenty-eight years old, I was too young to be an unrestricted free agent unless the Avs cast me aside during the summer. And they certainly could have disposed of me much more easily if I didn't choose one of their doctors to perform the surgery.

Faced with this pressure and the uncertainty of my future, I said okay to the Avalanche and decided to let their doctors attempt to fix my knee. In the short term it was a wise decision.

Following my knee surgery, the Avalanche gave me a two-year contract. The first year I would be paid $950,000, and the second year I would get $1.1 million. Considering the fact that I would be coming off major surgery, and therefore didn't really have any leverage, I was very happy to get two years and that kind of money.

That said, in the long-term view of things, it may have been a bad decision to let Colorado's team doctors perform my ACL surgery.

As the days after my surgery went by, I was still having problems with my knee. I needed to find some answers. My teammate Uwe Krupp had ACL surgery and did not have the kind of pain I was having. The pain was so bad that I ended up taking Vicodin for thirty-three straight days after surgery.

Vicodin is usually prescribed for people experiencing intense pain after surgery. It helps calm a person down and increases their ability to relax and forget about painful ailments, which speeds up recovery. Anyway, like I said, I was taking Vicodin for the pain. I'm not talking about taking just one a day, either. As soon as one wore off, I would pop another one because the pain was so intense. That kind of intense pain is just not normal in post ACL surgery.

Meanwhile, back on the ice, my teammates advanced to the Western Conference final after eliminating Edmonton in the second round of the Stanley Cup playoffs. This meant another date with the Detroit Red Wings in the conference final.

All along I'd been hoping to come back and play in the playoffs with a brace. Some guys are able to play without an ACL. It depends on your knee structure. Ray Ferraro, then playing for the Blues, tore his ACL during the 2003 Stanley Cup playoffs, but was able to keep playing in that series with a brace, before retiring over the summer. Ray still hasn't had his ACL repaired, even after retiring. He runs and works out all without his ACL. I am so bowlegged, playing with a brace wasn't going to happen for me.

After I had my surgery, I began traveling with the Avs during the series versus Edmonton and then Detroit. The team wanted me around, and I felt like I was still part of the effort in a small way. It probably wasn't the best thing for my knee. It wasn't feeling right, and I'm doing all of this traveling and moving around. Not smart.

It was hard watching the Red Wings beat us in the Western Conference Final knowing I could have helped. Scotty Bowman came up to me in the hallway one night and wished me well, which I thought was an extremely nice gesture.

However, as more and more people came up to me to wish me good luck, I started thinking, "Damn, maybe this thing doesn't just heal up and you come back and are the same guy." At that point I became really worried.

The ACL reconstruction that Avalanche doctors performed on my knee was the kind where they take the middle one-third of your patella tendon, roll it into a graft with a couple of bones on each end, and then screw it in under your knee. That's your new ACL. What normally happens is that this new man-made ACL is fine, which in my case, it turns out, it was.

So, my new ACL was good. But in that type of ACL surgery, doctors purposely create a second injury by taking the middle one third of the patella tendon out. Usually, this isn't an issue, because in 90 percent of the people who have this kind of ACL surgery, the middle one third of the patella tendon grows in again naturally, and there are no problems. But I had a major problem.

The middle third of my "injured" patella tendon did not grow back properly. In fact, it shrunk.

It felt like I had on a really tight sleeve that was holding my kneecap against my bone. There wasn't enough room for it to have a full range of motion. As a result of all of that, I couldn't build my thigh muscle (quad) back up again. Quad muscles shrink after knee surgery, and you need to build them back up again, especially if your job happens to be a professional hockey player. I couldn't build my thigh back to its normal size. The bone on bone situation did not allow for a full range of motion, and it was extremely painful.

Another way doctors often repair torn ACLs is by using donor tissue from a cadaver. This way, doctors are able to repair your ACL without touching your patella tendon. If doctors had performed this kind of surgery on my torn ACL, I probably never would have had a problem with my knee. So, in the end, the knee surgery performed on me was the wrong kind of ACL surgery.

For a while I blamed the doctors for the incorrect surgery that would eventually end my career and cause me issues and discomfort to this day. But I really don't play the blame game anymore. Whatever. Things happen. I was born the way I was born with my bowlegs and I'm the one who kicked out Eric Daze's leg on the play that got me injured anyway.

You beat yourself up over the decisions you make in life and sometimes that's just the way it is. Eventually, I got past that anger, angst and the shoulda, woulda, coulda.

But back then, it was time to survive.

CHAPTER 13
"DOCTOR, DOCTOR CAN'T YOU SEE I'M BURNING, BURNING"

My knee was never right again after the ACL surgery, and I never kept it a secret from anybody. I told every teammate, coach, G.M., trainer, and doctor that would listen that something wasn't right, because I was still convinced that there was a way to fix it. I didn't yet realize that I was screwed.

Eventually, after it became clear that my knee just wouldn't improve, I went in to see the Avalanche team doctor, Dr. Andrew Parker. My wife Laura came with me because, as she said at the time, "Everyone says you're fine."

It was a difficult time in my life. I had all these people counting on me as athlete, employee, teammate, and provider. And they were all looking at me and they were all saying, "What's wrong? The doctors say you're fine."

People around you think you are a mental midget or that you can't take the pain. I know some people doubted me when I said that my knee wasn't right and that it hadn't functioned properly since the surgery.

Even when I saw the doctor with Laura, he kept reiterating that everything was fine with my knee. He said that they would do one more little surgery, clean it up, and I would be good to go.

Despite how badly the first surgery went, I stayed with the same doctor. I'm a loyal person. If someone says they are going to help me, then I believe them. Unfortunately, my knee wasn't the only problem at the Avs 1997 training camp.

As I was dealing with a knee that didn't work, I also needed to get one of my teeth crowned. So, I left Colorado Springs, where we were training, and headed back to Denver. Herbie the dentist, aka Dr. Barker, put a crown on my tooth, and then I went back to Colorado Springs. Once the anesthesia wore off, I went to take a drink of water and proceed to immediately spit out the crown. The pain was unbelievable! I had just had about three hours of dental work done and I was thinking, "What the hell is this?"

So, there I was, I had no leg, everyone thought I was fine despite the fact that I couldn't even skate, and now I had this fargin' tooth to deal with. I was losing it. I raced back to the dentist's office and he takes one look at it and says I now have to get a root canal. Great.

I head over to a different office and sit in the chair for five hours getting a root canal. Near the end of the root canal, I hear this awful sound from the drill. Like it got jammed or something while he shaved the tooth down or did whatever he was doing.

I said, "What was that?!"

And he says, "You're fine, you're fine."

I'm like, "What?"

So, he finishes whatever he was doing, finishes the root canal and says, "You're fine."

And I'm thinking, "Really?"

So, I head back to Colorado Springs. A few hours later I take a sip of water and almost die again, the pain is so excruciating.

Well, now I'm pissed. I flip out and call Dr. Barker. He tells me to come to the office. So, I go back to Denver. I am in so much pain from this tooth, it is unreal. You can't imagine the pain. I get to Dr. Barker's office and he looks at it and says, "We have got to get this tooth out right now. It's abscessed underneath. "

This is my third day in a row of going back and forth from training camp in Colorado Springs to Denver. So, it turns out Dr. Frankenputz has to cut my tooth in half because it's so big. I can feel my jaw separate as he's trying to get this tooth out of its space. He pulls it out and it is the size of a cue ball. Freakin' ginormous. And he's like, "Okay, we got it."

So, I drive all the way back to Colorado Springs for what's left of training camp. I'm still trying to get on the ice while I'm dealing with this tooth thing. I am skating, trying to build up strength, but I have nothing. My brace doesn't fit and nothing is going right. I'm really down. I'm thinking my career is over. The team is telling me I'm fine and I'm thinking I'm going to have to retire because I'm so useless on the ice.

Meanwhile, back in my mouth, I have more dental issues. There's this thing called dry socket. Dry socket is a layperson's term for alveolar osteitis, a disruption to the healing of the alveolar bone following extraction of a tooth. Well, I develop one of these dry sockets and my mouth begins filling up with puss and stinking horribly. I'm telling you, it smelled like burnt hair.

For thirty straight days I have to go to the dentist's office and have the puss sucked out of this dry socket thing. I have this knee that won't get better and now this tooth problem. Finally, I lose it. "That's it," I say. I storm into the room and start screaming, "Parker and Barker, are you sure you two didn't get mixed up?! Maybe, you're the dentist and you're the doctor!" I liked both guys, but I flipped out of frustration.

Meanwhile, back at my knee, I had continued telling people something wasn't right to the point that the Avalanche thought I was nuts. But like I said, I knew something was wrong from day one and I knew even more as time went on. The 1997-98 season was about to start and I had to tell the team, "Look, I can not skate."

So, I went to work with Fred Stoot, the magician who had done wonders for my back and groin when I first got to the Avs. I worked with Fred while my Avalanche teammates began the regular season. I drove myself to Colorado Springs just about every day, and worked out for a minimum of four hours in an attempt to get some leg strength back. We did whatever we could to work around the pain and my limited range of motion in order to get some muscle back on my shriveled leg.

The then-named Pacific division wasn't very strong that season, and we eventually went on to win it again. But we had gone from winning the President's Trophy the year before, to finishing with the fourth most points in the West and seventh most in the NHL. We were not the same team. We were the second seed during the 1998 Stanley Cup playoffs by virtue of winning the Pacific Division.

During the long Olympic break in February of 1998, I went on a rehab assignment with the Hershey Bears in the AHL. Bob Hartley was the coach for Hershey at the time. He eventually became coach of the Avs, and won a Stanley Cup during the Ray Bourque Cup run in 2000-01.

Meanwhile, I was still playing on one leg. I made some progress with Fred Stoot, but there was still a major issue with my knee. I played four games in Hershey, scoring two goals and getting an assist, but it was a joke because I couldn't even skate. Still, I was deemed ready to go by the Avalanche. I would be coming back to the NHL on one leg.

The team continued to tell me that my knee would get better, but it stayed the same. It wasn't improving. I had no muscle.

I returned to the Avalanche and got off to a pretty good start, but I knew something was wrong. I played all but one game after the Olympic break, twenty-three games in all, and scored three goals and had seven assists.

One of the saving graces during that painful season was hanging around Jari Kurri all year. He was playing his final season in the NHL with us in Colorado. He scored just five goals in seventy games, but it was enough to get him his 600th career goal, making him one of just sixteen players to reach that accomplishment. Kurri would retire with 601 goals and 797 assists. We all called him "Jerry." He was a funny guy who told us stories from the old Edmonton Oiler days and we were all ears.

Well, I had this poster of all the 500 goal scorers in NHL history up to that point. I had gotten it at one of the many charity golf events NHL players take part in. I had gotten the autograph of every person on that poster (each signature right beneath the player's picture) except for two: Mike Gartner and Jari Kurri. It was really a cool item. Jari had scored his 500th as a member of the Kings in 1992 on an empty net. Here's some trivia for you; Kurri, Wayne Gretzky, and Mike Bossy are the only players in the 500 goal club to have scored their 500th career goal in an empty net.

Now that Jari was a teammate, it was the perfect time to get him to sign my poster (which was becoming more valuable with each signature). So, one day I went up to Jari and asked him if he would sign the poster for me. He says sure. So, I hand him this poster of all the 500 goal scorers, which at that point had 26 members. Well, Kurri's face just lights up. He looks at this poster like he is seven years old and it's Christmas morning. I can't get over the youthful enthusiasm that this man, who has done so much in his hockey career, is showing while looking at my poster.

So, I'm standing there, looking at him look at the poster, and I blurt out, "Why don't you just keep it?"

Jari responds, "Really?"

And I say, "Sure."

Well, the next day he overnights it to Mike Gartner, who signs and returns it, and Kurri takes it home with him to Finland after he retires at the end of the year. It's gotta be worth a nice chunk of change now, especially with all 26 signatures.

Anyway, back to the 1997-98 season. We were the second seed in the Western Conference, and played Edmonton in the first round of the Stanley Cup Playoffs. I still couldn't skate. On top of that, early in the series Mike Grier hit me from behind and I separated my shoulder.

Now I couldn't skate *and* I was getting needles inserted into my arms to alleviate the shoulder pain. In the mornings I could hardly crawl out of bed.

Shean Donovan was my roommate during those playoffs. He was a perfectly healthy guy. He was ready to play and could skate like the wind. I could barely get out of bed. However, the Avs wanted that name in the lineup, with the name on the back of the jersey, to play the way that name used to play before the injury. But Jones couldn't play that way with his knee all messed up.

We got up in the series, three games to one, and it looked like we would advance to the second round and play Detroit. That is, until we lost Game 5, 3-1, and Game 6, 2-0.

After Game 6, I went to Marc Crawford and said, "Crow, I can't help us. I can't play." I continued, "I will play for you. I will do anything you ask me to do. But, I'm killing us. I can't move. Don't play me."

Meanwhile, I had been called in by G.M. Pierre Lacroix and his then-assistant Francois Giguere earlier and told to be more physical. I kept telling them that my knee wasn't right. After all this time they still didn't and wouldn't believe that there was anything wrong with my knee. They replied that the doctors said my knee was fine.

With the series tied at three games each, Marc Crawford calls me the night before Game 7 and says, " Jonesy, I need you to play." I reply, "I'm there for you and I'll do whatever I can."

Well, we go out on home ice and get shut out by Curtis Joseph, 4-0. We outshot the Oilers 31-17. The Oilers became the fourteenth team in NHL playoff history to rally from a three games to one deficit, and in two of those instances I was on the losing end. I gave the best I had, which was nothing.

I was a minus one and had no shots on goal. I was a company man, playing physically and even getting a roughing penalty at 2:21 of the first period. One second after I stepped out of the box, Edmonton scored to make it 1-0. That's the kind of night, series, and year it had been for me.

Just like that, the 1997-98 season was over and I was like, "What do I do now?" I was practically crippled.

I went back to Michigan for the summer, and worked out for hours upon hours trying to find a way to build the muscle back up in my thigh. Eventually, I just blocked out of my mind all the stuff I had to do to get ready to play. I knew I had one year left on my contract and I was a little scared about what would happen after that. I couldn't even do a normal leg press, or any other normal leg exercises for that matter. I had to ride a stationary bike with a high seat to alleviate the pain in my knee. I needed to find a way to strengthen my leg if I wanted to stay in the NHL.

I got back to training camp for the 1998-99 season. There were days I made it onto the ice solely by trying different things to keep my knee in certain places just to make it work. Other days, I had to leave the ice I was in so much pain.

I was twenty-nine years old, and I said to myself at training camp in the fall of 1998, "It's over. I'm done. My NHL career is over."

CHAPTER 14
BRACE YOURSELF

Just when I thought there was no hope of finding something that would get my knee to a place where I could make it work, I got a new brace during training camp in the fall of 1998. All of my summer weight-room work had put a little muscle back on to my left quad, but I still needed something else to keep my knee stabilized. It would never have been strong enough on its own. The brace, plus my own ingenuity, finally gave me some hope.

My experimental mode began when I taped the new brace to my leg like a cast, so that I couldn't move anything. Nothing could slide. With everything immobilized, my knee was able to work. I began the 1998-99 season on the ice with the Avalanche.

We lost to Ottawa on opening night, but I made two assists and was off to a good start. We then got shut out in quick succession by both the Sabres and the Bruins. Each team beat us 3-0. Game 4 of the season we lost again, and suddenly we were 0-4. We tied the Los Angeles Kings on October 18, and were now winless in our first five games under new coach Bob Hartley. Marc Crawford had resigned the previous May.

The team was winless as we hosted the Edmonton Oilers, the team that came back on us the previous spring in the opening round of the playoffs. Little did I know when the game began that I would score one of the most unusual goals in NHL history.

It's late in the game and we're up 5-4. Claude Lemieux scored a couple of goals, including his 300th career. I'm on the ice in the last minute of the game, as the Oilers are going for the tying goal. The Oilers pull goalie Bob Essensa, and so their net is empty. I'm defending one of the points, so I'm doing whatever I can to chip the puck out of the zone, or to block a shot with any part of my body if the puck gets to my point.

The clock's winding down, and there are about fifteen seconds left as the puck comes to the right point in our zone. All I want to do is get down on the ice, block the shot and preserve our much needed first win of the year. When you get off to a bad start at the beginning of a season, the whole organization can get on edge real fast. Jobs are on the line.

So, I'm playing with this taped-on knee brace that looks like a cast on a skier's broken leg. Sure enough my homemade device comes in handy.

A shot gets blasted from the point and I go down to block it. I'm sprawled on the ice as the puck comes flying toward my encasted leg. Between my shin guard, knee brace, and hockey pants, I am pretty well protected, a veritable human racquetball court wall. The puck caroms off the wall of protective plastic around my knee like a rocket, and begins sliding out of our zone, through the neutral zone, into the Edmonton zone, and towards the empty Oiler net.

The sellout crowd watches the puck slowly slide toward the net and braces themselves for something they've probably never seen and will never see again: an NHL player scoring a goal on a 120-foot blocked shot.

The puck continues to slide. As I roll over on the ice and look up, the puck slides, and slides, and slides, and slides, right into the middle of the empty net. I mean, right in the middle. If it was one of those in between period score-o contests I definitely would have won a new Buick. My 86th career NHL goal. After what went on the year before, I didn't think I would ever get another one.

It was still slow sledding for the Avalanche in the early stages of the season. After thirteen games, we were 4-8-1 and on our way to Phoenix. I'd played eleven of thirteen games up to that point, and had two goals and two assists.

We flew to Phoenix to play the Coyotes, and when we arrived at America West Arena where they played, I walked into the dressing room and couldn't believe what I saw. There was my sweater in the locker with an A on it! Alternate Captain. David Poile was right! It wasn't a C, but it was close. The only time in my career I ever wore an A. So, I'm looking at the A and I'm NOT thinking, "Wow, what a great honor. I'm wearing an A in the NHL!" No, I'm thinking, "Shit, this is my last game! This is my last game for the Avs! They are trying to fool somebody tonight. But they can't fool me."

I'd been playing better the last few games and had begun to feel a little stronger on my skates. I said to myself as I looked at that A, "This is it! I'm done in Colorado. They're going to trade me." I was convinced that the A was all bullshit. Pierre Lacroix was playing with my head. Or maybe management was trying to inspire me. If I scored a hat trick then maybe they could squeeze a little more out of whatever team they were trying to trade me to.

Skating around warm-ups, I was screaming at Jeremy Roenick and Keith Tkachuk with a pronounced sarcastic tone, "Hey look at this boys! I'm the Alternate Captain! Woooooooo!"

I went out and played one of my best games of the year. I drew four penalties, skated well, and the brace was locked in. I had been hearing that there were some teams interested in me, so my trade intuition wasn't out of left field.

Actually, I had been thinking to myself that the only chance I had of continuing my NHL career was to get to a team that could help me with my knee.

I was thinking and hoping that a new team would fix the thing with my knee and we could get going again. At that point, I wanted to be traded and get with a new team and a new set of doctors. Maybe they'd see something that no one was seeing in Denver. I figured my career was done otherwise. I kept thinking to myself, "There's got to be a doctor somewhere who can help me with this knee." No one had told me that they couldn't fix it.

So, the game in Phoenix went well. I played pretty decently while wearing my "A," and the game ends in a 1-1 tie. A scintillating late 1990s NHL game, with two goals and a combined forty-six shots in sixty-five minutes of hockey.

We headed towards the plane to fly back home to Denver. We had two days off until our next game, a home game against a bad Tampa Bay Lightning team that would go on to finish with the worst record in the NHL. Two days off + next game at home versus a bad team = someone is getting traded or fired. I was convinced that I was the one who would get traded after seeing that A stitched on my sweater.

As we boarded the plane, everyone was in their dress code uniform of suit and tie. Except for me. I walk on the plane with a pair of blue jeans and a tee shirt. I walk right by the coaching staff and all the players. I sit down and start playing cards and Patrick Roy takes one look at me and says, "What the hell are you doing?!"

I say to Patrick, "I'm done. I know I'm getting traded so screw it. This is what I'm wearing now."

Because of my knee pain, I carried my gigantic brace with me everywhere I went. It was called a protonics brace. A knee brace for joint stabilization. It was supposed to be active resistance therapy for improving patellofemoral congruence and eliminating patellofemoral pain. Kneecap jargon. But, it kept some of the pressure off my knee, was a useful tool for keeping everything aligned, and it kept me playing. When the guys skated during morning skates, I put on my brace and walked around the visiting arena in my warm-up gear. It helped to align my hips and enabled me to play that night. I carried that big ol' brace around with me wherever I went. If another NHL team ever saw me carrying that huge knee thing around they never would have traded for me!

So, I have this big brace with me on the plane, I'm in jeans, and no one wants to mess with me because I'm so nuts at this point trying to get this knee better. Coach Bob Hartley walks right by me on the plane. And doesn't say a word.

We arrived back in Denver and Marc Crawford called me. Crawford had begun the year working in television after resigning from the Avs after the previous season. He wound up taking over in Vancouver later in that season.

So, Crawford asks me, "How are you doing? I got some teams calling asking me about you. Are you able to play with your knee the way it is?"

I say, "Crow, I think I'm fine. I think I'm coming through this thing. I got a new brace now. I'm stronger on the ice now and I think I can pull this off."

I don't want to disappoint and bullshit Crow. I say I "think" I can do this.

He says, "Good, I think you are going to the Flyers."

Nothing happens the first day back from Phoenix. As I mentioned, there are two days before our next game. A home game against the Lightning.

On the second of our two off days, I drive to practice. I get there a little early, so I scan through the newspaper I bought on the way. I sit there in the practice rink parking lot, look at the Sports section and there it is. "Keith Jones traded to the Flyers for Shjon Podein."

I say to myself, "Oh, really?"

It must be true, it's in the paper!

I walk in the practice rink and into the dressing room and say, "Hey boys what's up?"

And they are like, "Ahhh, nothing. What's going on?"

I say, "I don't know. I read in the paper I've been traded. You guys hear anything?"

They go, "What? We don't know. We didn't hear anything."

I say, "It's right here! I got traded to the Flyers."

It was all so surreal. I went to the trainers room and got my regular treatment for my knee. Then I got in the hot tub with some different teammates and said again, "Did you see in the paper I got traded?" They all looked at me like, "What in the hell is he talking about?"

What was happening behind the scenes was that the Flyers' doctors were poring over all the info on my knee. They knew that my ACL was torn and were making sure that everything looked good. As you know, my ACL was fine. What they, or anyone else for that matter, including me, didn't know was I had a bad patella tendon, and that was causing all of my problems. It didn't, and wouldn't, show up on any tests. No one saw it. If they asked me to run three feet, I literally couldn't have done it. I hadn't run one day of my life since my first ACL surgery. My knee wouldn't let me do it. I could skate a little bit, but I couldn't run. I was a professional athlete who actually couldn't run. I played for five years in that condition. I also couldn't broad-jump two feet. Earlier in the year, during training camp, I didn't do any of the physical tests that were asked of me. Whenever I was asked to do something, I just said, "No, can't do that. Not doing that." No one came near me.

I went about my business in the practice rink even though the newspaper said I'd already been traded to Philadelphia. I started putting my practice gear on and prepared to go out on the ice.

I was sitting beside Patrick Roy in the dressing room, and he said to me, "Jonesy, why do you want to be traded?"

I replied, "Well, Patty, I'm not playing here. I have a chance to go to the Flyers and play with Lindros and LeClair. Here I'm playing the fourth line."

I was feeling a little more confident in my knee having played two pretty good games in a row. I was pretty sure I'd come up with a system for getting my knee ready. Taping on that knee brace like a cast and playing a couple of good games, and the 'ole Jonesy mojo was coming back.

I said to Roy, "I think it's my last chance to try and go do something productive."

Roy replied, "Well, we need you here. I don't understand why you want to be traded."

I told him, "Patty, I don't know if it's just about me wanting to leave or them wanting me to leave."

"I wish that wasn't the case," he said.

Just then, someone came in the room and said Pierre Lacroix wanted to see me. I looked at Patrick and smiled.

Unlike the time I was traded from Washington to Colorado, I didn't make the mistake of walking up with one skate on. I took all of my gear off and walked up to Lacroix's office.

I sat down and Pierre said, "We've traded you to the Flyers."

I said, "I know, I read it in the paper."

I thanked Lacroix for everything. He said Bobby Clarke, Flyers G.M., wanted to talk to me right there in Pierre's office. I said sure and got on the phone with Clarke.

So, Clarke says, "Hey, Jonesy. We got a game tonight in Florida. There's no way you can make that, but we'd really like to have you in the lineup tomorrow against the Devils."

"Hey, Bobby, you might want to rethink that," I say. "Have you ever seen my career numbers against the Devils?"

He goes, "What?!"

I say, "Why don't you take a look at those stats and see how badly you want me to show up for that game."

Clarke starts laughing and I start laughing, but my stats were no laughing matter.

I had played the Devils twenty three times in my career at that point, and had no goals and only three assists.

I got the flight information and headed out that night, November 12, 1998, to Philadelphia. Once we landed, I got word that the Flyers had just lost another game. This one to the Panthers, 2-1. After starting the year 4-0-1, Philadelphia had gone 1-6-3 in their last ten games.

There was an off day the next day, so I had a chance to practice with my new team. Roger Neilson was the Flyers coach then, and he said to me, "We are thinking about putting you on the line with Lindros and LeClair. We're trying to find a guy to play with them on the wing. I don't know if you are the right guy or not, but we might give it a shot."

I listened to Roger's uncertain analysis of the situation, and then said flatly and matter of factly, "Just put me out there, Roger. Put me with Lindros and LeClair and don't worry about a thing."

The old Jonesy was back. Filled with confidence, mischief, and ready to roll in Philadelphia.

CHAPTER 15
TIME FOR ME TO FLY

I played my first game as a Philadelphia Flyer on November 14, 1998. The Flyers were 0-5-2 in their last seven games, just 1-6-3 in their last ten, and needed a spark. The game was tied 1-1 after two periods and I had just gotten my skates wet with my new team and my new linemates, Eric Lindros and John LeClair. Our line took the opening face-off of the third period and at the end of our shift, forty-five seconds in, Lindros passed the puck from the left face-off circle into the slot, where I fanned on my first attempt. I then spun and sent a sliding backhander past Martin Brodeur for a 2-1 lead. My first goal ever against the Devils.

We went on to score four more times in the third period, out shooting New Jersey 17-2, and we won my first game in a Flyer uniform, 5-1. I had a goal and an assist, Lindros had two goals and three assists, and LeClair had two goals and one assist. What a way to start my Flyer career. I'd gone from begging for a goal off of my shin guard in Colorado to playing with these guys in a new city.

Right from the time I first arrived in Philadelphia, I got great massage work from the Flyers' masseuse, Tom D'Ancona. He loosened up the IT band on the side of my leg to give my kneecap more room. Tom worked endless hours on me. Those people love helping the players. John Worley, Jim McCrossin, and his entire staff put in long, hard hours getting me ready to play while I was in Philadelphia. Taping the brace and massaging my leg was helping me to move and allowing me to get in the right spots to help out those two great players, Lindros and LeClair.

Our next game was in Pittsburgh, where I scored the first goal of the game and we won again. I was pointless the following game against Carolina, but then in Florida I scored the winner twenty-six seconds into the overtime. Prior to the winner, at the end of regulation, I blocked a shot in attempt to keep the game 1-1. The puck hit me directly on my bad left knee. I had gone down on both knees like I was praying in the direction of the point man. When you do that, the part of your shin guard that goes over the knee cap comes away from your body a bit. Well, that happened and the puck hit me right on the kneecap. I said to myself, "Here we go." Being in the last year of my contract, I couldn't get hurt again. I was lucky the last time to get a multi-year deal after tearing my ACL.

I walked it off in the locker room after regulation, trying to get some life back into it. I sucked it up and got back on the ice in overtime. Lindros found me open again, and I scored the game winner. The only overtime winner of my career. My knee was still killing me. That night, my knee swelled up like a cantaloupe.

Even after two days of rest, my knee was still killing me after taking that slap shot off it in Florida. I couldn't play against the Islanders on November 25, my knee was too swollen. We went out and lost with me on the sidelines, so the boys started calling me "Moses." I played, we won. I sat out, we lost. They also called me Moses because I hardly practiced. Roger Neilson was great, giving me time off when I needed it. He left it up to me. If I had been with a physical fitness coaching nut who skated us every day, I would have been done for sure. Roger gave me my space. The best part about the whole not-practicing thing was that everyone thought I was just joking around. I played along and said, "I just play the games, boys!" But, my knee really couldn't have handled practicing and playing. I only had so much left under my kneecap. There wasn't another coach in the NHL who would have let me do what I was doing. One day a newspaper guy took a picture of me in a lounge chair, with a big cigar in my mouth, while the rest of the guys were practicing.

So, the doctors put a needle into my gigantic, swollen knee and drained it. So much blood came out that I was thinking, "What is going to happen?" But, as soon as they drained it, my knee felt great. It was back to where it was before I got hit by that puck. Sure enough, after one game on the sideline, I got back in the lineup against my boyhood team, the Maple Leafs. I scored halfway through the first, and had two assists, and we won 1-0. After a game off, we won again 4-3, and I had a three-point night. "Moses" was back! I was so relieved after having been in that gray area of, "When is my knee going to go and when am I not going to able to play anymore?"

Still, I approached every game like it was my last. That desperation, and the fact that I was playing with those two human cyborgs who seemed to do whatever they wanted on the ice, had me playing well. And we were winning. Eric Lindros and John LeClair were so good and so dominant at that stage of their careers, that it didn't matter that I couldn't skate as well as I used to. As good as the players were in Colorado, Lindros and LeClair were in a different world. They were just amazing down low and complemented each other perfectly. As a result, I didn't have to do as much. I just had to get them the puck and get to a spot. With my knee in the condition that it was in, it was the perfect place for me. For all the bad luck I had had up to that point, the trade could not have worked out any better. It was absolutely a fortunate move for me.

By then, I was experienced and smart enough to know where I needed to be on the ice, and I was getting there a little bit quicker because the whole knee brace experiment continued to work well. I didn't have to be that fast, I just had to get there. Plus, I was still good along the boards. I had enough stability with the brace that I wasn't getting knocked off the puck along the boards. I couldn't hit like I used to, but I could still handle myself. I just had to map my way to the net, because I couldn't afford to get hit on my left side. I had to shoot off my right leg all the time as well, because my left was so weak. You just adapt.

This was all great luck because it was the last year of my contract making $1.1 million. I was begging every night just to make it through the season, get another contract, and continue my NHL career. I knew that I probably had only one more contract in me. Amazingly, on my dicey knee, I played 12 games with the Avalanche and 66 with the Flyers for a total of 78 games that season, tied for most in my career. Playing with Lindros and LeClair, I went on to score 18 goals in my 66 games with the Flyers, and finished the season with 20 goals, 33 assists, and 53 points. I was also a plus 29. A long way from my minus 7 game with the Baltimore Skipjacks.

Lindros and LeClair scored 40 goals each. They were attracting so much attention that I was left open a lot. Playing the third wheel with players like that, you have to be doing something right. Lord knows I couldn't carry anybody else, but playing with those guys, I fit. You'd think anyone could play with two top guys, but that's not the case. It's an important job, and one I was made for at the time.

The city of Philadelphia made me feel great my first year as a Flyer. I felt at home right away. The adrenaline was really flowing and I was feeling better and better, so I was able to hit again and stir the pot — all those things Philadelphia loves. Every time I hopped over the boards with Lindros and LeClair, there was a buzz going through the arena. It was an awesome time.

I knew most of the fans' love was for the two big guys with all the goals, but I definitely felt like they also embraced me and my role. They made me feel great about myself. I went from thinking, "What am I going to do with my life?" to getting my career high in points.

Then the playoffs arrived and we opened up against the Maple Leafs. It was the always exciting 4-5 opening round matchup. We were the fifth seed. As a result of Eric Lindros' injury, we were the under-dogs. Eric was training, trying to come back after recuperating from his collapsed lung surgery in Nashville. With Eric out of the lineup, Rod Brind'Amour was playing a lot. Only Eric Desjardins was playing more.

We went out and won Game 1, 3-0 with goals by LeClair, Zelepukin, and Desjardins. John Vanbiesbrouck made 25 saves for the shutout. Part of my job became helping to shut down Mats Sundin and Steve Thomas in even strength situations. Sundin had 31 goals that year and Thomas had 28 during the regular season. After them, the Maple Leafs didn't have a lot of firepower. If we stopped Thomas and Sundin, our chances of winning the series would be pretty great.

So, to try to stop Thomas, I did what I did best. I tried to drive him nuts. My linemates and I did a great job. We held the line to one point in the series. Roger Neilson, who had a reputation for being a very religious and upstanding man, said to me before the series, "Jonesy, do you have any dirt on the Maple Leafs? One year we had a guy who had some dirt on people and it really helped! Do you know anyone sleeping with anyone or anyone drinking too much?" I told Roger that I didn't have any salacious breaking news, but I still wouldn't have any problem stirring it up. I respected Steve Thomas a lot. I grew up a Maple Leaf fan, and I had just turned seventeen when Thomas played his first full season in the NHL with Toronto. That was 1985-86. Thomas was in the NHL while I was playing Junior C hockey for the Paris Mounties. Thirteen years later we were playing against each other in the Stanley Cup playoffs and my job was to make him hate me to take him off of his game.

In Game 2, I was playing with Daymond Langkow and Mark Greig, and I scored at 11:09 of the first period to give us a 1-0 lead. It stayed that way until late in the game. We had a chance to go up two games to none. I wasn't on the ice when Steve Thomas tied the game with 1:59 left in the game. Or when Mats Sundin scored with fifty-three seconds left in the first overtime, while I was watching from the bench. We lost 2-1, and the series was tied at one. Toronto won Game 3, 2-1, on a power-play goal by Steve Thomas forty seconds into the second period. Toronto only got off eight more shots on goal, but held on to win the game. We exploded for five goals in Game 4 to even the series at two. With it all tied up, the series shifted back to Toronto for Game 5.

There we are in Maple Leaf Gardens. I'm playing on a line with Mikael Anderson and Marc Bureau and we are on the bench since Sundin, Modin, and Thomas are on the ice. Well, we go in and I score 1:52 into the game. Man, does that feel good. Scoring a Stanley Cup playoff goal in Toronto for the second time in the series. Unfortunately, Dimitri Yushkevich scores later in the first to tie things up at one and Yanic Perreault scores in overtime. The Maple Leafs take a 3-2 series lead. Game 6 in Philadelphia. A must win for us. It's a defensive struggle with very few shots on goal. After two periods, we are outshooting the Maple Leafs 18-14. In the third period, with 2:54 left in the game, referee Terry Gregson calls an elbowing penalty on John LeClair. Well, the 19,706 Philadelphia fans go nuts. As does our owner Ed Snider. This is the "old" NHL. To get a penalty at the end of Game 6 in a Stanley Cup playoffs in 1999, you usually had to stab someone in the eye with a rusty knife. Terry Gregson's call was definitely against the grain. Looking back, it sure looked like the right call. But again, at the same time, it seems outlandish to call a penalty in such a big game. Well sure enough, Sergei Berzin scores a power-play goal with exactly one minute left, and the Maple Leafs win the game and win the series.

So, we head back to the dressing room and everyone is livid to lose a playoff game, and a series, in such a fashion. Well, Mr. Snider, whose passion is unbelievable, comes down to the room and says to me, "Say whatever you want about Gregson, Jonesy! I'll pay the fine!" So, I blast Gregson in the media and get a $1,000 fine from the NHL. Roger Neilson also blasts the officiating ref in his post match press conference. At the same time, outside our dressing room, Mr. Snider questions Gregson's integrity. A few days later, as we're cleaning up for the season, Mr. Snider says to me, "Well, you didn't get it as bad as me.

I had to pay $50,000!" Roger Nielson was also fined $25,000 for publicly criticizing the officials. I'm sure Ed Snider paid that fine, too.

Everybody loved Ed Snider. You will never hear a bad thing from anybody about him. He was so passionate about the game.

He had such a gigantic presence, yet made you feel like such a part of the organization. It wasn't a country club in Philadelphia. You were there to perform. As long as you worked, you were a Philadelphia Flyer. If you didn't, you wouldn't be for long.

Ed Snider became wealthy because of the Philadelphia Flyers, so you won't find anyone who appreciates the game like he does. Mr. Snider was the son of a successful grocery-store-chain owner. On February 8, 1966, the league awarded Philadelphia an NHL franchise, one which would eventually be named the Philadelphia Flyers and start playing in 1967, the year before I was born. By 1971, Mr. Snider had become owner of the Spectrum, where the Flyers, as well as the Philadelphia 76ers, played. In 1974, he created a management company to run the Flyers and the Spectrum, called Spectacor. Spectacor would found or acquire several businesses under Mr. Snider, including a regional premium cable channel, PRISM, and an all-sports radio station, WIP. Founded in 1987, WIP is where I now work, hosting the "Morning Show" with Angelo Cataldi and a cast of few.

After my strong season, and the productive playoff series against the Maple Leafs, I signed a three-year, $5 million contract with the Flyers. My knee was holding up and I was still convinced there was something out there that could bring it back to where it once was, because no one ever told me it was unfixable. How could something in such a small area keep me from playing more in the NHL?

CHAPTER 16
LIFE SAVER

I truly believe Eric Lindros meant well. For us players in the dressing room of the Philadelphia Flyers, most of the Eric Lindros drama was outside of our walls and in the newspapers. Like everybody else, we read things in the newspaper about Eric's parents and the Flyers' front office. Like anything else, some of the wild rumors were probably true, and some of them probably were not.

Eric had no intention of bothering people in Philadelphia. He went out of his way to talk to, and be nice to, kids and the fans. He was great that way. I was his roommate on the road and linemate on the ice, and that was an interesting place from which to view everything that swirled around him. The way I look at Eric Lindros is that he was a big help in extending my career. With the condition of my knee and the quality of my skating, I needed to be carried by two great players, and Eric Lindros and John LeClair did just that.

No. 88 was an extremely talented player who put a lot of pressure on himself to be great. He was reserved and quiet and didn't talk about all the weight that was on his shoulders. The expectations were so high for Eric to take the entire NHL to the next level, and there were times when he did. I know from playing with him that he was a phenomenally talented player. There were several occasions when Lindros and LeClair absolutely dominated the opposition to the point of physical exhaustion. That was fun to be a part of.

I can see why, even if the front office had problems with him and his family for a long time, they still kept Eric on the team. He was that good. He was huge, he was strong, he practiced hard, he worked out hard in the gym, and he played hard. No one could question his work ethic. Ever.

Should he have been captain? Sometimes captains are these powerful, emotional leaders. That wasn't Eric's way. He led by example in terms of how hard he trained, practiced, and played. And Eric Lindros really wanted to be captain. I think he really liked it and believed it meant something. Was he a great captain? I think there were better ones.

Sometimes Eric would get in trouble with the third- and fourth-line guys because he demanded, and received, so much ice time. They looked at that as selfishness, and they believed he was putting personal goals ahead of the team's success. There was a time when coaches played the hell out of their top lines and that would have been my instinct, too. But teams that were winning Stanley Cups were playing four lines. Mike Modano, Peter Forsberg, and Joe Sakic, just to name three, recognized that they needed all four lines to win. Eric demanded to play, and I think that's where some of the resentment might have started from a player's standpoint. We were a top-heavy team in terms of minutes played, and that's not the best thing for team unity and chemistry.

But in terms of not living up to the massive hype that was shoveled upon him, injuries were the underlying reason he didn't achieve everything that was expected of him. And, of course, when you look at his numbers, they are still awesome. He had twenty-two goals in his first forty-three playoff games with the Flyers. Better than a goal every other game in the playoffs is incredible. He played so physically. No other great player played like he did. Other guys who had played similarly physical games, Neely, Forsberg, and others, eventually kept getting more and more injuries. They weren't meant to play a long time at a high level. In fact, if you look at Cam Neely's career numbers and those of Eric Lindros, they are very close, and Neely is in the Hall of Fame. Plus, Eric has a Hart Trophy on his résumé.

As my first season with the Flyers was winding down, we headed to Nashville for a game with the Predators on April Fool's Day. Lindros

*There is something incredible about wearing a
Flyers uniform and stepping on the ice at home in Philly!*

had just served a two-game suspension for a high-sticking incident against the New York Rangers the previous week, and this was his first game back. He was having another monster year, and the game against the Predators, would be his 71st of the season. He should have had no problem eclipsing his career high for games played in a season. At that point, he had had just one known concussion in his career, and that had been over a year ago when he was hit by Darius Kasparaitis and sidelined for 18 games. His previous high had been 73 games played, and we had seven games to go in the 1998-99 season.

Up to that point, No. 88 had forty goals and fifty-three assists for 93 points. He was continuing to build a young and bulging Hall of Fame résumé. So, we go out and beat the Predators, 2-1, on Rod Brind'Amour's twenty-second goal of the season. Eric plays 21:16 and everything seems pretty normal, although he complains of some pain in his ribs. I play with Eric and John LeClair for most of the game, while the second line is Brind'Amour centering Mark Recchi and Mikael Renberg. That line accounts for both of our goals.

After the game, Lindros looks a little uncomfortable and I ask him what is the matter. He says he has pain in his chest and rib area. He gets some ice and electrical stimulation after the game, but still feels some soreness. He feels okay enough to head out with the boys for the night.

So, we all shower and go out for a couple beers and a burger there in Nashville. Eric still isn't feeling well, so he just has a Diet Coke and heads back to our room at the Renaissance Hotel. Meanwhile, Recchi has been battling concussion problems, and while we are out his arm goes numb right there in the restaurant.

So, Mark leaves early as well, gets nauseous, and calls our trainer, John Worley. They go to the hospital for the night, where Mark gets a CAT scan. Later that night, I head back to our room to go to bed. Eric is still awake, watching a movie and not feeling well. I ask him if he wants a couple of Advil, he says yes, and I give him a couple. Then I go to sleep.

A couple of times during the night, I hear the bathtub running. I don't think much of it, because sometimes hockey players will hop in the tub to try to give their bodies some relief. I just assume that's what Eric is doing. The next morning, I get up and ask him how he's doing, and he says his ribs still hurt. I say, "You look really pale."

He says, "Yeah, I don't feel good."

I say, "I'll call John Worley." So, I call Worley's room, but he isn't there because he's at the hospital with Recchi.

Meanwhile, Eric is getting worse and so I call Worley again. I finally reach him around 7:30 or so in the morning. He has just gotten back from a sleepless night at the hospital with Recchi. He says he just wants to clean up, and he'll be up to the room after getting his bearings back. I know John is going to come and see Eric, so I go down and have some breakfast in the hotel. I come back up and Eric is back in the tub, pale and in even worse shape than he had been. I say to him, "Something is wrong here. Maybe it's something internal. I'll go get John right now. I think we got to get you to the hospital."

So, I go to find Worley. As the elevator opens, John is there on his way to our room. Meanwhile, the team is getting ready to leave for Boston. So, I take Eric's stuff down to the bus, and that's the last I see of anybody in Nashville.

While we're heading to Boston, they take Eric to Baptist Hospital in Nashville. When we land in Boston, we find out that Eric punctured his lung in the Predators game, and it had since filled with blood and collapsed. He had surgery in the emergency room. Later, it is determined that if Eric had flown with us to Boston, he could have died. Who knows?

His condition is so bad, there's no way he's even going to get dressed and drive to the airport, much less get on the plane. After his surgery, when it was clear everything was going to be fine with his health, Eric holds a news conference.

The first thing he says is, "I want to thank Keith Jones for saving my life."

Did I save his life? I don't know. I just noticed he wasn't looking good and left it up to the medical staff to take care of it. I got a lot of credit for something I'm not sure I deserved. I guarantee you everyone's intentions were to make sure the right thing was done to help Eric. What was already a bit of a circus involving Eric and the Flyers inflated to Big Top status.

As players, we just went about our business. Eric was hurt and you moved on. That's what you do in professional sports. As players, we didn't talk about injuries or injured players because we were only one hit away from having something happen to us. So, as a result of his punctured right lung, Eric missed the final seven games of the 1998-99 regular season, and the playoffs as well.

CHAPTER 17
"HEY, THAT'S MY SCHTICK"

Our next game after the Lindros/Nashville bathtub incident was in Boston on April 3. We were playing a pretty good Bruins team that was on its way to making the playoffs. The B's were a 91-point team that season, and would go on to win a playoff series against Carolina in the opening round before being eliminated by Buffalo in the conference semi-finals. That was the last playoff series the Bruins won, and the only playoff series they've won since the lockout of 1994-95.

1998-99 ended up being Ray Bourque's last full NHL season in Boston. At the time, the very idea of him playing for another team seemed absurd. Ray Bourque playing for any team other than Boston was as unimaginable, as Joe Sakic playing for anyone but the Avalanche, Mike Modano playing for anyone but the Stars, or Steve Yzerman playing for anyone but the Red Wings. However, the Bruins were awful the following season, finishing last in the Northeast Division. Seeing little hope for a team that could contend, and being on the back side of thirty, the Bruins Captain and civic institution asked for a trade with the hope of finally getting his name on the Stanley Cup before he retired to the finest golf clubs in North America.

Many, including Bourque himself and all of us in Philadelphia, were hoping the legend would end up becoming a Flyer. Bourque wanted to be traded to Philadelphia because it was so close to Boston and his family, and he knew the Eastern Conference so well. I remember talking with my teammates about getting Bourque the following season. As the deadline was approaching, we played a game against the Bruins, and out on the ice, we kept telling him, "See you after the game, Ray!" We really thought we were going to get him in a Flyer uniform, and we believed that if we did, he would have been the final piece in bringing the Cup to Philadelphia. But it wasn't meant to be. The following year, #77 would be in Colorado playing and striving for his first Stanley Cup with the Avalanche. He didn't get it that first spring in Denver. They lost to Dallas in the Western Conference Final, while we lost to the Devils in the Eastern Final. The following season would be Bourque's last. Cup or no Cup. Playing in what he and his family knew would be his final NHL game, Bourque won his first and only Cup in the spring of 2001 when the Avs beat the Devils in seven games. Without me!

Despite having been only a couple of years removed from the team, I wasn't bitter or resentful, and didn't feel like I had missed out on something. I was rooting for my friends in Colorado. I had always looked at being traded as proof that I was wanted, which is always good for the self-esteem. Thinking back to playing Juniors, when no one really wanted me for so long, always gave me a kick whenever I pulled a new NHL sweater on over my crooked nose. A fresh sweater always smelled good, and it always felt good. It always felt like I was wanted and that I had a new opportunity to be in a better situation. Philadelphia was, and is, the perfect situation for me. Then as a player, and now as a retired player/broadcaster.

As we took the ice in Boston that early April day in 1999, our team was obviously in a bit of a daze due to everything that had happened with Lindros the night before in Nashville. In fact, we went on to lose the next two games by a combined score of 8-1 as we regroup from yet more drama surrounding our captain. We did regroup, and won three of the remaining games of the regular season, losing one and tying the other. The loss occurred in overtime against the Devils when Bobby Holik scored the winner. Meanwhile, I scored my 20th goal of the season in the second period of that sold out game. I had two goals for the Avalanche when I was traded for Shjon Podein on November 12. I scored 18 for the Flyers in the 66 games after the trade. The

78 games I played that year are tied for the most I ever played in one season in my life. Little did I know, my NHL hockey career would be over after just 65 more games.

The goalie for the Bruins that Saturday afternoon in Boston was Byron Dafoe. Dafoe was having his best season in the NHL. He went on to win 32 of 68 games that season with a body, like mine, built more by Tim Horton doughnuts than by Bowflex. We weren't quite Chris Farley in that disturbing yet hilarious Chippendales tryout sketch from *Saturday Night Live* that you see on NHL Jumbotrons, but we were close.

"Bysie" had an amazing 10 shutouts, 1.99 goals against average, and .926 save percentage for the Bruins that year. He finished third in the Vezina voting, after runner-up Martin Brodeur and winner Dominik Hasek, who won his fifth Vezina in six years. Hasek would win his sixth and final Vezina two years later, one shy of the Vezina record of seven held by Jacques Plante. Plante won his Vezinas when they were given to the goalie, or goalies, who gave up the fewest goals in a season. That changed in 1982, after which the best goaltender was determined by a vote of general managers. I imagine the Bruins didn't vote for Dafoe so he would have less leverage in any future contract negotiation.

Bysie was always such a great guy. We started together for the Baltimore Skipjacks late in the 1991-92 season. I had just come from Western Michigan and Bysie had finished up playing Juniors for the Portland Winter Hawks and some ECHL hockey for the New Haven Nighthawks. I was taken in the seventh round of the 1988 draft, and Bysie was drafted the next year by the Capitals in the second round, thirty-fifth overall.

Whether it was game day or not, Bysie was always engaging and a great teammate. I actually think that in today's NHL, he would be a good fit. He moved well and was athletic. Like me, leg injuries did him in. We both retired from the NHL at age thirty-three.

Anyway, the afternoon game between the Flyers and Bruins in Boston begins, and we actually have a good first period, outshooting the Bruins 13-7. Sergei Samsonov scores the only goal of the first, beating John Vanbiesbrouck. From there the game gets slow and defensive. We only get eleven more shots on goal the rest of the game, and the Bruins get just thirteen more. Real high quality entertainment for the 17,565 in attendance, and the national TV audience watching on ESPN 2. The Bruins should have had autographed-Ambien-day for the first 10,000 fans. It would have had the same affect.

Now, for some reason, nothing is going right for me. There are times when my mind just isn't focused right, and this must be one of them because I'm in La-La Land. I'm third in minutes played this day behind Rod Brind'Amour and Mikael Renberg, yet during my 22 shifts I am 0-1 in faceoffs and have just one shot on goal, two measly hits, no penalties, no takeaways, no giveaways, and no blocked shots! I'm a human pylon. I don't think I even face wash anybody. To be fair, my teammates aren't doing much better. Dafoe could have gotten his shutout asleep in a recliner with a half eaten cruller on his chest.

We are in the third period and everything that could possibly go wrong for me is going wrong. Not the least of which is the fact that for the third time in the game, I lose my stick. I'm battling with Anson Carter, and my stick just comes loose and falls to the ice. I say to myself, "That is enough!" So, I rip Carter's stick out of his hands. I'm sure I was able to get it out of his hands so easily because it's something you just don't anticipate when you are playing hockey. Anyway, Carter is stunned. You expect your stick to get grabbed now and then, but not lifted like a wallet in broad daylight. The last time I stole something was shoplifting when I was twelve. That incident scared me so much that to this day, I can't take two *USA Today's* out of a newspaper vending machine. However, on this particular afternoon in Boston, I'm so bored I suffer a sudden relapse of kleptomania.

In 1999, the NHL still used a one referee system, and apparently referee Terry Gregson bypassed La-La Land and proceeded directly into post-lunch lady nap land. There is holding the stick and then there is stealing the stick. Well, as Gregson is struggling with his sudden case of narcolepsy, I say, "Screw it, I'm going to play with Carter's stick!" At the same time, a switch goes off in my mind and I'm like, "That's it, I've had enough!" I'm more pissed at myself for not being able to hold on to my stick all day.

Sure enough, the puck comes to me behind the Bruins net. Now, Anson Carter is a right-handed shot, and I am a left-handed shot. Imagine Phil Mickelson stealing Tiger Woods' lob wedge and playing with it on the 18th hole of the Canadian Open. So, here I am trying to stick handle with a stick curve designed for a right-handed shot yet still playing left-handed. As circumstances have it, I end up stick handling around the net and all the way up toward the defensemen at the blue line.

Meanwhile, Carter is screaming at Terry Gregson, "He has my stick! It's right-handed!" So, I start laughing at the first entertaining thing to happen all afternoon. I can't stop laughing as I continue my shift playing with Carter's right-handed stick, left-handed.

Apparently not one to be outdone, Carter picks up my stick, which is left handed of course, and starts playing right-handed with it, which is even funnier! So, the shifts goes on for what seems like forever (although it's probably only twenty or thirty seconds) and referee Gregson is looking at me like I have a zit on my nose or something. The Bruins and Ray Bourque are screaming that I stole — and am now playing with — Carter's stick. The whistle finally blows on an offside, and both teams make a line change. Our bench is on the far side of the ice since we were in the Bruins zone and it was the third period. So, I skate diagonally toward our bench and, right in the middle of the gigantic spoked B in the center of the ice, I drop Carter's stick behind me and continue on empty handed. At this point, Terry Gregson and his linesmen, Gerry Gauthier and Brian Murphy, realize what happened.

Fortunately or unfortunately, depending on your point of view, all of this is caught on national television on ESPN 2 with Darren Pang providing the color. In an otherwise drab game, this is the most enjoyable shift. As I approach the bench I have a little smile on my face, but can't laugh too loudly because we are losing 3-0 late in the third period. I come back on the ice the next shift and Ray Bourque is just looking at me, smiling and shaking his head over what went on with Carter's stick the shift before. I don't know Ray at all at the time, but I'll never forget the sly look he gives me that shows he saw the humor in it.

It was one of those rare moments in the NHL when the lighter side came into play, even though we were losing 3-0. We were playing pretty well all year and so it was the perfect time to get away with something like that and add some levity to our sometimes tense team.

CHAPTER 18

"HEY, THAT'S MY PLUS"

Gearing up for training camp for the 1999-2000 season, I was feeling pretty good. And truth be told, I had plenty of reason to. I had just come off a plus 29 season, during which I scored 18 goals in my 66 games with the Flyers. Furthermore, I had played well in our playoff series against Steve Thomas and the Toronto Maple Leafs. Off the ice, and this is a big one, I had just signed a brand spanking new three year contract that would pay me $1.5, $1.7 and $1.8 million a year for the next three seasons. Kelly Miller money! I also hit the 400 NHL career-game mark during the 1998-99 season, which got me a full retirement pension. And last, but certainly not least, the Flyers were looking like Stanley Cup contenders in the upcoming season.

Now, I had spent the previous months in Ann Arbor, Michigan, just as I had spent the previous couple summers, trying to get my knee stronger. For the most part, that meant riding a stationary bike to stay in shape and to try to build up some knee strength. I still had to put the seat up real high to limit the range of motion. This helped to alleviate the pain from the bone-on-bone friction that was going on in my knee.

Roger Neilson was still the coach in Philadelphia at the time, and his training camp tradition was a 25 mile bike ride in Peterborough, Ontario. You see, Roger's coaching career began in 1966, when he was the head coach of the Ontario Hockey League's Peterborough Petes, then a junior farm team of the Montreal Canadiens. He kept a home there until his death in 2003.

In preparation for Roger's training-camp bike ride, I had ridden my stationary bike at 25 miles a session throughout the summer, and I

154

was fine. I could do it. Now, little did I know, when you ride a bike on a real road, there are times when you need to stand up in order to pedal the bike up a hill. My knee would never allow such forceful pedaling.

Well, we're up there in Petersborough, about to begin this 25 mile bike ride, and I say to Craig Berube, "Hey Chief, we'll ride together." Before I begin, I take the seat on my bike and adjust it a bit higher. I figure everything will be fine without realizing, of course, that I will have to stand up at some point to pedal up the steeper hills.

Guys are leaving every 30 seconds, and when it's my turn, I start peddling. Well, there is a big hill right at the get-go. I'm still straining up that first hill 45 seconds later, and here comes Craig Berube who had started thirty seconds after me.

"Where are you going, Chief?" I ask.

He says "What are you doing?"

I say "What do you mean?"

"You're not moving" he replies. I think I'm pedaling fine, but I can't stand up, so I'm moving at a snail-with-a-pulled-groin's pace. I end up riding 25 miles of hills sitting down on my ass. By the middle of my ride, everyone who had started after me has passed me already, except for one guy. I look behind me and here comes goaltender Neil Little of the Philadelphia Phantoms. I say to myself, "Oh my god, it's getting worse."

Meanwhile, my knee is burning beyond belief. But I keep telling myself, I have to finish this bike ride. Then I see the Jeep that goes around giving people water and I try to flag it down to rescue me. Well, because of my reputation as a clown, they think I am kidding and they drive right past me laughing. Most guys finish the 25 mile ride in about 90 minutes or so. It takes me two hours and 45 minutes. Because of my reputation, no one seems to really care, or ask if there is any kind of problem with me. It's just Jonesy being Jonesy.

After the ride, everyone is at Roger's house in the pool and hot tub, having a good ol' time, while my ass is burning and my knee is swollen and on fire. I finally get my turn in Roger's hot tub, sit down and say to myself, "I think I'm done." My knee feels completely wrecked. Roger Neilson's bike ride has ended my career.

The next day we are on the ice and I turn sharply on my swollen knee and tweak something in there. Sure enough, I have to have arthroscopic surgery at the end of training camp. The doctors go in and clean out all of the debris that has been collecting as a result of the bone-on-bone friction that occurs everyday of my life, and was exacerbated by the twenty five mile bike ride. I miss the first 25 games of the season after rehabbing for two months.

My first game back was on December 2, 1999 in Buffalo. I only had twelve shifts, and played just over ten minutes. I managed to pick up a double minor for roughing after tangling with noted enforcers Miroslav Satan and Dixon Ward. Two nights later in Montreal, I played a couple more shifts and picked up a slashing penalty in a win over the Canadiens. We won again in my third game back, but my ice time was under ten minutes and I only got on the score sheet for an elbowing penalty early in the third. Now I knew what it felt like to be a third- or fourth-line guy watching Eric Lindros and Mark Recchi play so much. But, we were 3-0 since I came back, and I was on fumes with my knee, so it was all good. Game number four was against the Toronto Maple Leafs on a Thursday night in Philadelphia.

Now, let's go back for a second to the previous spring and our playoff series loss to the Toronto Maple Leafs. The man who I had successfully badgered, Steve Thomas, is about to shake my hand in the ceremonial handshake line that ends every Stanley Cup playoff series. Many have waxed poetically about this grand display of model sportsmanship. Well, after taking my physical and verbal abuse throughout the series, Thomas grabs my hand and says, "I swear on my kids' head, I'm going to kill you in the first game between us next year."

To be fair, I had really given it to Stumpy all series long, including breathing on him with my famous garlic breath. You see, I used to eat a big thing of garlic bread with assistant coach, and hockey legend, Wayne Cashman before every game. Incidentally, I have to say here that I really loved Wayne Cashman. I was all ears every time he told us stories from his days with the Big, Bad, Bruins. Of course, it didn't hurt that he once went toe to toe with Jim Schoenfeld in a Zamboni entrance. But I digress. Like I said, Wayne and I would eat a bunch of garlic bread, and I would let my breath get good and stinky. Come gametime, I'd lean on Thomas during face-offs, get real close to him, and breathe my dragon breath all over his face. I'd also jam my stick between his legs, rub my stinky glove in his face during scrums, and do anything else I could think of to try to get him off his game. I did a pretty good job at it, too, and that is why his handshake came complete with a death threat.

Now, my teammates knew about the comment Thomas had made in the handshake line the previous spring, so they were looking forward all season to a confrontation on the day of the big match-up. Well, that day had arrived.

Prior to the game, my buddy Craig Berube keeps calling me, saying things like, "That Thomas is going to kick your ass today! You're going down!"

And I keep telling him, "I don't care, Chief, I'll fight him."

We keep going back and forth.

"Bullshit! He's going to kick your ass!"

"No way, man, I'll fight him!"

Well, the game begins and Toronto starts Steve Thomas, which is expected. Roger Neilson figures I did a good job against Thomas the previous playoff series and send me out to start against him and his line. Like me, Thomas plays right wing as a left-handed shot. He's better at it than I am, though. He's had a couple of 40-goal seasons, and goes on to retire with 421 goals. At this point, he is a thirty-six-year-old winger winding down his career, and this will end up being his last 20-goal season.

So, Thomas is on his side, and I'm on mine, and we're looking across at each other as the puck drops to start the game. Forty seconds into the shift, Thomas slashes me to provoke a fight. Here we go. My first regular season fight in almost three years. The last one was against Todd Simpson when I played for the Colorado Avalanche.

Thomas and I drop our gloves. I figured I'd keep a defensive posture, and just try to hang on. Maybe get a shot or two in. Well, I did manage to land a couple of punches, and before I knew it, the fight was over. And I wasn't too much worse for wear. A wise-ass to the end, I skate past the Toronto bench on my way to the penalty box and yell over, "Who's next?!"

Well, my bout must have inspired the boys. Eric Lindros goes on to get a hat trick, and my boy Craig Berube has a scrap with Tie Domi. We win 4-2.

The season continued and my playing time remained at a low level, deservedly so. I was just hanging on. I played 57 games in the 1999-2000 season, scored just nine goals and had 16 assists.

While I was dragging myself through 57 rather unproductive games on a deteriorating knee, the Flyers had a good season. We amassed 105 points, the most in the Eastern Conference. Mark Recchi led the team in scoring with 91 points, while John LeClair played in all 82 games and led us with 40 goals. We had six players play at least 80 games, and a total of nine played at least 70. Two people who were not healthy were Eric Lindros and I. Eric played in only 55 games, and like I said, I played in only 57. I was ready for the playoffs, however, and Eric was not. He was out with his third concussion of the year after colliding with the Bruins' Hal Gil in early March. We finished the regular season by winning four games in a row, five of six, and eight of eleven. Craig Berube scored the last goal of the season against the Rangers, to cap off a 4-1 win. It was an empty netter with ten seconds left.

We entered the 2000 Stanley Cup Playoffs playing well, despite not having Number 88. My knee seemed to be holding up, too. In fact,

I had just recently scored my 117th and final regular season NHL goal. It happened on April 6, against the Atlanta Thrashers, when I scored on that noted fitness guru Norm Maracle (who, incidentally, may have been the only guy in the league with a worse body than me). I was playing on a line with Peter White and Valeri Zelepukin, and they both got an assist. To be fair, the Thrashers were by far the worst team in the NHL that year. They were the only team that didn't break the 50 point mark. In fact, the Thrashers were so bad they didn't even break the 40 point mark. They finished with 39 points, and won only 14 of 82 games that year.

Our 2000 postseason began against the Buffalo Sabres on home ice. Like any team, we were excited to be in the post season and had great anticipation. Our team was really coming together, and the bond we were creating is one that I still cherish to this day. But, as opposed to my days in Colorado where players constantly verbalized winning the Stanley Cup, we were a little hesitant to start talking Stanley Cup in Philadelphia. Buffalo had Dominik Hasek, and we had a rookie goalie in Brian Boucher. And even though we were the first seed and the Sabres were the eighth, some people considered the Sabres the favorite.

I beat Hasek in a power-play with eight seconds left to score the first goal of our post-season run. At least that's what history says.

The puck actually never touched me. Daymond Langkow shot the puck and I was screening. The puck never hit me, but they gave me the goal. After the game Daymond said to me, "Just keep it old man. You're just about done anyway."

How right he was.

We played good defensive hockey the rest of the game. I can't take a whole lot of credit, however, because I played just 10:31. Craig Ramsey, on the other hand, can take a lot of credit. He was behind the bench for Roger Neilson, who was battling cancer at the time. Craig was the best assistant coach I ever had. He was a brilliant hockey man with tremendous attention to detail. His personality wasn't ideal for an NHL head coach, however. Simply put, he is too nice of a guy.

Anyway, we held Buffalo to just twenty shots on goal and won Game 1, 3-2. Game 2 was the very next night, and I felt it. No shots, no hits, two minor penalties. One of those minor penalties occurred when Hasek and I met up in the corner. Hasek went to play the puck, and I decide to run him. My thoughts regarding penalties was to take them early and with a purpose. We knew we had to get in Hasek's kitchen and rattle him if we wanted to win the series.

So, anyway, I run Hasek and the Flyers fans go nuts. I'm on top of him, grabbing his mask, and screaming in his face, "YOU DON'T WANT IT AS BAD AS WE DO!"

Hasek and Patrick Roy were the best goalies in the net at the time. But, Hasek had a weakness. We knew we could exploit his emotional side. If you ran Roy and took a penalty, it wasn't going to rattle him. If anything, it might even make him play better, as Jeremy Roenick once found out.

Game 2 was the one where John LeClair scored the "game winner" through a hole in the side of the net. At the time, we definitely thought the puck went between the posts. We didn't find out until afterwards, when the reporters pointed it out. Don't forget, that was the second time in three post-season games that Sabres fans got the shaft. The previous spring, the Dallas Stars won the Stanley Cup in Buffalo on Brett Hull's controversial, skate in the crease, Cup-winning goal.

So anyway, we won Game 2, 2-1, and were in control of the series. Despite being up 2-0, there still wasn't a great sense of winning a Cup. Even still, when the series shifted to Buffalo, we played a great road game and won, 2-0. Brian Boucher posted the road playoff shutout. Also, it bears mentioning that I ran Hasek for the second straight game. Flyers fans still come up to me and talk about my back to back runs on the Dominator during the 2000 Stanley Cup Playoffs.

It was telling to me that none of Hasek's teammates backed him up after I ran him, especially on home ice. One of the Sabres should have pounded me. I certainly would have pounded someone if they ran Brian Boucher. I let Hasek know the rest of the series how much his teammates "hated him." Once again, I was the epitome of an NHL pest. There are so many ways to be a contributor to your team besides scoring goals. And for me, as my career was winding down and I was scoring fewer goals, being a good pest helped me to remain an important part of the team. The Buffalo series is a good example of how valuable a pest can be. By picking the right opportunity, early in the game, to run him, I was able to rattle Hasek, and reveal fault lines in his team's dynamic.

The series was basically over, as we were leading three games to none, so Craig Ramsey rolled four lines in Game 4. We held them to 17 shots on goal, but Stu Barnes scored the winner in overtime, and we lost. We rebounded in Philadelphia, however, for Game 5. Brian Boucher outplayed the Dominator, and we held the Sabres to just 22 shots and won, 5-2. Having built their team around Hasek, the Sabres had won plenty of games with only 20 shots on goal. But they didn't that night.

After playing five games in eight days and eliminating the Sabres, it was nice to get a week off. I felt fine. I mean, my knee issues were at least manageable at that point. I actually would have preferred to be playing games every other night. It was easier to prepare that way.

Up next were the Pittsburgh Penguins, a strong team whose playing style stood in sharp contrast to the defense-minded Sabres. The Penguins went 37-37-8 during the regular season, and had finished seventh in the Eastern Conference. That said, they had only scored four more goals than we did, and they had given up 57 more. This was going to be a good match up for us.

We went out and lost the first two games of the Penguins series at home. In Game 1, we held them to just 14 shots on goal, but lost 1-0 on a winning shot by Jaromir Jagr. I played only 9:14 of the game.

In Game 2, we managed to fire off 45 shots on goal, but got "Tagnutted" by the Penguins' goalkeeping phenom and lost 4-1. Jagr scored two more goals, which put him at three for the series. Meanwhile, I only played 8:35 and had zero shots on goal.

On the bright side, I did pull off a hat trick of roughing penalties in the third period. The most memorable of the bunch was my center ice fight with Bob Boughner. There are Bob and I, exchanging punches and pleasantries, when all of a sudden he goes down like a ton of bricks. As much as I'd like to take credit for a devastating knockout blow, that wasn't quite the case. Luc Richardson had had control of the puck, and saw the two of us going at it. Realizing there was no way he'd be able to get there in time to save my ass, he fired off a 90 mph slapshot that whizzed past me and drilled Boughner right in the chest. The next thing you know, he was down on the ice, gasping for air. That was Luc. He was the ultimate teammate. He actually had to explain to the NHL what had happened, and managed to convince them that he was merely trying to dump the puck.

The whole escapade was just another example of how close we were becoming as a team during the 2000 Stanley Cup Playoffs. We really would have done anything for one another. And even though we were down two games to one, as Luc's life saving slapshot showed, we would never give up, and we would fight for each other.

The series shifted back to Philadelphia for what was practically a must-win Game 3. We really dominated that night, out-shooting the Penguins 44-18, and I had my best game of the playoffs. I came out in the first period and had three shots on goal, made an assist on Andy Delmore's opening goal, and then scored one myself to make it 2-0. I didn't have any more shots on goal after the first period, but I did have a take away. That was a feat in itself, especially considering that at that point in my career, I was more or less moving like a trash can. On that night, however, I had good jump.

Unfortunately, Jagr went on to score two goals, his third and fourth of the series, and it was all tied up. The game went into over-time, and we were down two games to one. We had to win.

Our desperation really showed in OT. We out-shot the Penguins 11-1. At 11:01 into overtime, Andy Delmore scored the winner, and I had one of the assists. In a must-win playoff game, I was able to muster up a goal and two assists. On the road, no less. We were back in the se-ries, though still down by one, and getting ready for what would turn out to be a playoff game like no other.

My role on the team evolved in Game 3. We were down two games to one, and we didn't have Eric Lindros, who was out due to an injury. Meanwhile, Jaromir Jagr had scored five goals in the first three games of the series, and we needed to shut him down if we wanted a chance of winning. And so that became my focus. I was playing mini-mal minutes at that late point in my career. I wasn't on the ice for power plays, or to kill penalties, so my primary concern was to cover Jagr during even game situations. Easier said than done. At that point in his career, Jagr was a beast on the ice. He was 28 years old, and very much in his prime. At 6′2″ and 230 pounds (a full 60 pounds of which was likely accounted for by his ass), and possessed of incredible leg strength and lightning quick hands, Jagr was nearly unstoppable. You just couldn't get around him. Despite playing in just 63 games, Jaromir won the scoring title for the season, and his fellow NHL players voted him best player of the year with the Lester B. Pearson award. So yes, I had my work cut out for me.

What's more, I wouldn't be able to fall back on my talent for be-ing a pest. Having played against Jagr numerous times back when I was on the Capitals, I knew that he had learned to play along with the likes of me, and even give as good as he got. As much as I tried to verbally abuse him, he would keep his cool for the most part, and even come back with some really good one-liners. I'd be on a power play with the Capitals, and Jagr would lean over the bench say, "what are YOU doing out there?!" It wasn't always like that, of course. In his first few years in the NHL, he didn't understand pests like me. Players would be on him relentlessly, every second of every shift, and it would have the desired effect of getting him off his game. But those days were gone.

Now, Jagr had me worried, but he didn't have me that worried, mind you. First of all, I had never played on a team before where the players all looked out for one another like the Flyers did that year. Guys like Rick Tocchet, Keith Primeau, Luc Richardson, John LeClair, and Craig Berube set an example every night. And as Luc had so handily demonstrated with his sniper job on Boughner, we had each others' backs every game. Also, by that stage of my career, my role and time on the ice was so diminished that I didn't prepare for games night in and night out like I used to. At that point, I'd pretty much just show up at the rink and be like, "whatever."

For that reason, I didn't let it get to me that I wasn't as well rested going in to Game 4 as I could have been. So I didn't have the best pre-game nap? Big deal. I was like, "lets have a couple of cups of coffee and let's go." It turns out that Jagr wasn't in the best shape either. He missed the pre-game skate, claiming he didn't feel well. The stage was set: the tired guy would be covering the sick guy.

Well, Game 4 gets underway and don't you know, the Penguins score on the first shot of the game. Alexi Kovalev gets an assist from Robert Lang to beat the Langkow-LeClair-Recchi line 2:22 into the first period. It's 1-0, and I'm preparing to twiddle my thumbs and play my ten minutes with Peter White and Valeri Zelepukin, when a couple of our guys, including Simon Gagne, get banged up. Little wonder, too. The referees that night are Dan Marouelli and Rob Shick, and they might as well have been practicing triple toe loops out there on the ice. It's classic NHL 2K hockey. That is, clutch, grab, violate, pull, turn your head and cough hockey. And Marouelli and Shick only call 11 penalties all night long.

Anyway, with several injuries now upon us, I realize I'm going to be playing more than ten minutes. I turn to Craig Berube and say, "I better have another cup of coffee. It's going to be a long night." Little did I know.

Fast forward to the third period. Jagr is playing a lot. In fact, he goes on to play 59:08, so he must be a quick healer. But it isn't a full recovery. His flu-like symptoms are wearing him down, as is the virus that is my stick to his gut, and he's playing listlessly. He isn't the major force that he usually is, and the fact that I'm hanging all over him isn't helping any. Looking back, my little tango with Jaromir was typical of everything that was wrong with the NHL in 2000. The fact that a guy like me with one leg could eliminate the threat of world-class player like Jaromir Jagr simply by clutching and grabbing just wasn't right. Anyway, it was what it was, and that night at least, Jagr was more or less neutralized.

Clutching and grabbing may be something you can get away with in 2000, but slashing, for the most part, isn't. Martin Straka gets a penalty for just that 4:43 into the third period, and four seconds later John LeClair scores on the power play to tie the game at one. The referees review the goal to see if he tipped the puck while his stick was above the crossbar. Considering the fact that Johnny Vermont has recently been credited with a goal that went in via the side of the net, we remain confident the goal will stand. And it does. No one scores the rest of regulation, and tied up at one, the game goes into overtime.

Going into overtime, we are obviously desperate. We're fighting for our lives, and meanwhile the Penguins smell a 3-1 series. It is fairly action-packed, for 2000 anyway, and there are 14 shots on goal combined. In a game where the Penguins fail to get double-digit shots on goal during any single period, that isn't bad. It's actually one more than the combined shots on goal for the third period.

Anyway, we go back to the dressing room after overtime, and I am hungry. And I don't mean hungry for victory, although I was certainly very hungry for that too. No, I'm hungry for food. All I have really had in my system the last five or six hours were those cups of coffee. For a guy who typically plays ten minutes a night, playing twenty minutes, and on an empty stomach no less, is a major shock to the system. Especially when that guy isn't in the greatest shape to begin with.

In the second overtime, each team gets off seven shots on goal. Not a single one gets past Ron Tugnutt or Brian Boucher. Tugnutt will actually go on to make 70 saves in Game 4, only the second time in his career he performs such a feat. No slouch himself, Boucher makes 57 saves.

We make our way back to the dressing room after the second overtime, and by now everyone is hungry. Caveman hungry. So, we order some pizzas. The pizza arrives, and there I am, sitting with my shirt off and my gut hanging out, stuffing pizza into my piehole. I tell my teammates, "Don't worry boys, I'm like a bear hibernating in the winter. I've got enough fat stored up to get me through 50 overtimes! I'm worried about you poor bastards with 3% body fat. Just get on my fatback, fellas."

The third overtime begins, and before long, I jump on the ice for a line change. I skate in to the neutral zone, and watch as the play goes from our blue line to their blue line and back again. The defenses are playing a back-and-forth game of chip-it-out/bang-it-off-the-boards hockey. So I'm standing there, not moving, watching the puck go back and forth like I'm at Wimbledon. As this is going on, I skate all of three feet, proceed to get winded, turn to the bench and scream, "CHANGE!!"

Well, I manage to drag myself off the ice, and the third overtime dwindles to a close. In the dressing room, the guys continue to eat pizza. Some of them are actually on IV machines to replenish their fluids and relieve the fatigue. Even still, when the fourth overtime begins, we are all past the point of exhaustion. Everything is happening in slow motion at this point. It's totally surreal. Six periods of old style NHL hockey, with all of the clutching and grabbing to fight through, tends to have that effect.

Somehow, in the fifth overtime, I get a second wind. We are eleven minutes in, and I jump down on the ice for what turns out to be one of my longer shifts of the night. For the first time in the game, I can actually feel my legs underneath me. Who knows, maybe I'd just never realized that my knee needed a good seven and a half periods to warm up. Or perhaps all of this skating has finally gotten me in shape. Either way, I'm flying around the Penguin's zone, and our line is sustaining some serious pressure. In a final burst of energy, I rifle a shot at Pittsburgh's net. It's just wide, and the Penguins are able to clear the puck. I'm thinking, "Man, I just used up everything I've got. I have to get off the ice."

Meanwhile, Luc Richardson retrieves the puck from behind our net, and is looking for the breakout. He moves it up along the boards, and I come back as quickly as I can for some support. I am so spent, all I want to do is chip Luc's pass out of the zone and far enough down the ice so I can get to the bench. I take a swat at it, and send the puck out toward the neutral zone and in the direction of the Penguin's net. At the same time, Keith Primeau comes off the bench and heads towards Pittsburgh's zone.

Seeing my chance, I make a move towards our bench, which is conveniently located diagonal from me on the opposite side of the ice. Egypt seems closer at this point. Primeau is moving in on Tugnutt, but I'm not even watching the play at this point. My head is down, I'm gasping for air, and I'm just hoping that Primeau chips the puck deep, so I don't get stuck out there before I can make it back to the bench. Just before I arrive, Rick Tocchet gets up and climbs over the boards to replace me. A little bit to early. Then, the rest of the guys jump up and start climbing over the boards. I'm thinking, "Oh my god, we're going to get a 'too many men on the ice' penalty!"

It isn't until I look down the ice and see the guys hugging that it dawns on me that we must have scored. Remember, the game is in Pittsburgh, and only four or five thousand people are left in the arena. When Primeau scores the winner, there isn't a sound. Later on, I would see the highlight of the wicked wrist shot that Keith slipped over Tugnutts shoulder. The poor guy made an incredible 70 saves, and still lost the game.

Anyway, I have to skate over to the pile to get in on the celebration, but I'm almost too spent even for that. Almost. I eventually make it over, and converge on the celebration hug with the rest of the guys. I end up next to Tocchet, the guy who was coming over the bench to replace me on the ice, and give him a nudge. The first words out of my mouth are, "Hey, that's my plus!"

Game 4 of the 2000 Eastern Conference Stanley Cup Semi-Finals was the third longest game in NHL history. The first two happened in 1936 and 1933, respectively. That was back when they were still using brooms and human skulls to play, which made it much more difficult to score. So, I say our game was the longest. One of the best parts of that historic, five overtime game was the fact that the Flyers presented all of us players with a framed, commemorative game sheet. It was really thoughtful of them, and I was very pleased to be reminded that in the single most exhausting game of my life, I hadn't accomplished a single thing. In my 46 shifts (which totaled 37 minutes and 50 seconds) I had zero shots on goal, zero face-offs, zero penalties, zero giveaways, zero takeaways, zero hits, and zero blocked shots! Should you ever find yourself wondering if you ought to retire from professional hockey, I have a bit of advice. If your team presents you with a framed game sheet from a historically long match-up, and your stat line is completely empty – I mean, totally blank – than the answer is, yes, yes you should.

Of course, I was too thick headed to follow my own advice. I hung that game sheet right up in my basement, where it remains one of my proudest mementos, and got ready for the next game. I'm glad I did. The team was really coming together, and we won Game 5, 6-3, and Game 6, 2-1, to advance to the Eastern Conference Finals.

I have to say at this point that that was a pretty amazing feat, especially when you consider that we had gotten that far without Eric Lindros. Earlier in that season, Eric had gotten off to a good start. He was 26 years old and in the prime of his life. However, in late December, he got the second recorded concussion of his career in a hit from Calgary's Jason Weimar. Consequently, he missed two games. That was only the beginning of what has to be one of the most bizarre seasons in NHL history. A couple of weeks after the Weimar incident, Lindros was hit twice during the same shift in a game against the Thrashers. He missed four games from that one. Then in March, he was checked by Boston defensemen Hal Gil, and got his third known concussion of the season. He went on to play a few games before missing the rest of the season, and said that the team's medical staff didn't treat his injury seriously enough. As a result, Bob Clarke took his 'C' away, and named Eric Desjardins the new captain. Then, on May 4 – the very same day that we won the five-overtime game in Pittsburgh – Eric collided with Francis Lessard while practicing with the Philadelphia Phantoms farm team. That made four known concussions for the season. He missed the entire first two series of our post-season, and would make only a brief appearance during the third and final one.

Now, the 2000 Eastern Conference Finals pitted us against our archrivals, the New Jersey Devils. The Devils were a 103-point team that season, finishing only two points behind us in the Atlantic Division, and scoring the second most goals in the NHL, behind the Detroit Red Wings. Well, we went out against what was obviously a tough team, and lost Game 1, 4-1. New Jersey had gotten off to a strong start, and led 3-1 at the end of the first. To our credit, we held them to only eight shots on goal the rest of the game, four in each period. For myself, I played only 13:40, and didn't get much done.

We answered the Game 1 loss by winning the next three games in a row.

In Game 2, I played 16:27, had an assist, and was a plus 2. In Game 3, I broke a 1-1 tie in the first period with my third goal of the post-season while playing on a line with Keith Primeau and Rick Tocchet. We won Game 4, and took a 3-1 lead in the series, when Craig Berube scored the go-ahead goal with 7:02 left in the game. Everyone was cheering on the bench, and I looked over at Rick Tocchet and said, "That's all well and good, but what in the hell is he doing on the ice in the third period!"

That's how it was in those days. Our team chemistry was outstanding, and we were having a blast. Everyone felt like they were contributing. We knew we had a really good thing going, and felt like destiny was on our side.

Unfortunately, we returned home with a chance to cinch the series and advance to the finals, but fell behind early and lost 4-1. At the time, rumors began swirling that despite a Texas hat trick of concussions (that's four, for you Yankees), Eric Lindros would return for Game 6. Well, he did. He played well, scored, and had another one disallowed. But we lost 2-1.

You would think that adding a player of Eric's caliber was a no-brainer, no pun-intended. But I really believe that Eric's return changed the dynamic of the team, and not for the better. It's nothing against him personally. You see, we were a team of underdogs who really felt like it was us against the world. Our veteran group wanted to prove that we could make it to the Stanley Cup final with what we had. It didn't really have anything to do with the fact that it was Eric Lindros. The return of someone of his stature just altered the perception that we were a team that would have to defy all odds. We lost the little-old-engine-that-could mentality, and felt pressure to live up to the expectations that Eric's return inspired.

Anyway, the series was evened up at three. You can imagine what this was like for me, having already been on two teams, the Capitals and the Avalanche, that had blown 3-1 leads. Sitting in the back of the bus on the way home from New Jersey, I said to myself, "Here we go again."

I needed to get my mind off of the possibility of blundering a 3-1 lead, and the other guys did, too. So, we stopped for some beers on the way home. We ended up drawing power play diagrams on cocktail napkins, trying to figure out how we might pull it all off. So much for getting our minds off of things.

Our hotel bar strategy session yielded some good ideas, though, and at the morning skate before Game 7, my teammates urged me to talk to the coach about our lines. Now remember, the previous December Roger Neilson had been diagnosed with bone marrow cancer. He ended up having a successful stem cell transplant a month before the playoffs began, and received medical clearance to return to the bench for the Devils series. The Flyers, however, decided not to shake things up, and kept Craig Ramsay behind the bench. Like I said, Craig was the best assistant coach I ever had, but he didn't have the personality of a head coach. So, the veterans on the team pretty much ran the show. I know he resented our interfering at the time, but Craig respected my thoughts, and he knew how in tune I was with the other guys on the team.

So, I go into "Rammer's" office with Wayne Cashman. We're standing there, and in my first career game as an NHL coach, I say, "We got to move things around here." I give Craig my instructions for make-up of the lines, and then I tell him, "Luc Richardson and Dan McGillis should play against the Jason Arnott line. They played with them in Edmonton and know them. Maybe we'll get an advantage."

Fast forward to that night. Lauren Hart belts out "God Bless America," and Game 7 begins. I'm reunited on a line with Eric Lindros and John LeClair. Early in the first period, Patrik Elias scores on a power play, making it 1-0. Shortly thereafter, Ramsay sends me, Lindros, and LeClair back on the ice. Eric is all fired up and wants to get the game back to all square. He gets the puck just outside our zone with barely 12 minutes left in the first period, turns to his right, and starts barreling through the neutral zone, staring down at the puck like there was a picture of a swimsuit model on it. I'm behind Eric at the time, like I usually am given his speed and agility versus mine, and I'm screaming "Get your head up! Get your head up!"

Well, there goes Eric, flying across the Devils' blue line at top speed. And here comes Scott Stevens, leaving John LeClair wide open on the wing. And drilling Lindros right in the head with his shoulder pad. Down goes Eric. If he had had his head up, his amazing agility and substantial size would have helped him to absorb the hit, and he could have slid the puck over to a wide-open John LeClair, who would have broken in on the net alone. But Eric was a bull in a china shop, and he just went full steam ahead.

We can't retaliate. Jumping Stevens is not an option because it's Game 7 and we are down 1-0. People will say that we didn't do anything because it was Lindros, but that isn't the case at all. The building is silent, and it's eerie watching Eric leave the ice in that state. But the team responds fine. We had been playing and winning without Eric for the last sixteen playoff games, and a good chunk of the regular season as well. We were underdogs before, and now we are underdogs again. Far from being a shock to our system, we go on to play our best game of the series!

We come out in the second period and outshoot the Devils, 15-8. Three of shots are mine. At 6:01 into the second, Tocchet ties the game at one. This really gets us going, but we aren't able to get another one past Martin Brodeur. It's the end of the second period, and the game is tied up at one.

The third period is another one of those classic late 20th century NHL games. Clutch, grab, violate, repeat. There are eight shots on goal combined in the third period, both for us and the Devils. Of course, no penalties are called. The period is winding down, and overtime is looking likely. There's just over two minutes left when Elias scores again. The Devils win, 2-1. It's the third time I'm on the losing end of blown 3-1 lead. Not a happy hat trick.

As we're skating off the ice, Wayne Cashman puts his arm around me and says, "Well, you got your first loss, son."

"What do you mean?" I ask, confused.

Cash responds, "Your first coaching loss."

Looking back, it's really amazing that we went that far. My teammates and I, who had grown so close, went through a hell of a lot together in that crazy month and a half. There were some stunning triumphs. Beating Hasek in the opening round, the five-overtime game in Pittsburgh, the three game lead against New Jersey. And of course, there were some painful defeats. Man, was it painful blowing that 3-1 lead.

More painful, even, than my knee. Which, at that point, was on its last leg.

CHAPTER 19
MEET THE FULKERSON ...
THE END

The 2000-01 NHL season was set to begin, and my knee was killing me. I cleared waivers twice over the summer, but I was getting nervous again about the life expectancy of my NHL career. I was sensing the end, all the while holding out hope that somewhere out there in the wilderness was an answer to the riddle of the pain in my knee.

In all fairness to Flyers team doctor, Art Bartolozzi, he was given only my knee to examine. And there was nothing that feeling or moving in my knee would indicate any real problems. All the tests showed that my ACL was strong, and so it was assumed that everything in my knee was strong. Of course, I knew that that was not the case.

The season began and I had nothing. On opening night, we beat Vancouver, 6-3. I played 11 minutes and had two shots on goal. Then things turn bad. We went 0-5-2 in our next seven games. I played 7:28 in Game 2 of the season. In Game 5, I played 13:12 and was a minus two. In Game 6, I played 10:07 and was a minus 3. In Game 7, I played 9:28. We hosted the Ducks in Philadelphia for Game 8.

During the game against Anaheim, I went fishing for the puck with my feet when Duck defenseman Vitali Vishnevski drilled me, knocking me out cold. Now my overall health was in danger because of my useless knee. I couldn't even get out of the way of a slow moving Russian defensemen.

I had zero points in eight games and I was a minus 5. I was plagued by intense jets of pain shooting from my knee and up into my quad. And now I was concussed, largely due to a knee that wouldn't let me move.

I went to Flyers Assistant G.M. Paul Holmgren and asked him if I could get a second opinion on my knee. I knew there were big problems, and I was dying to find out the culprit. I still thought it could be fixed. Holmgren gave me the name of a doctor in Hartford, Connecticut that he knew from his days with the Hartford Whalers. His name was Dr. John Fulkerson. Fulkerson had been a doctor for U.S. Olympic Ice Hockey team, the NHL Hartford Whalers, and the AHL Hartford Wolfpack. Homlgren told me to go to Hartford and meet the Fulkerson. See what he had to say.

So, I head to Hartford with my latest MRI, which shows that my ACL is in perfectly good condition. I drive up to the building and limp inside to meet Dr. Fulkerson. The doctor looks at all the information concerning my knee. After sitting in his office for five minutes he turns to me and says, "Do you like golfing?"

I say, "Sure, I play a few times a year."

And he says, "That's good, because you'll have a lot more time to play now."

I'm like, "What?"

And that's when he drops the bomb on me. He says, "I can't believe that you can walk around on this knee. This is not a fixable thing. How have you been doing what you have been doing? How have you been playing professional hockey?"

At this point, I actually want to reach out and hug Dr. John Fulkerson. He is the first person to confirm that which I have been saying all along: this knee ain't right.

Fulkerson was a specialist in patellofemoral pain, and knew exactly what I was going through. He knew that my shriveled patella tendon was causing problems that couldn't be fixed, and that the bone-on-bone pain which prevented me from building up my quad would never really stop hurting. There was no way I could ever be a functional NHL player again. He gave me a full report on the condition of my knee, and I drove back to Philadelphia.

I knew that I would have to retire from the NHL, and on November 21, 2000, I did just that. Twenty-six years to the day after George W. Bush was honorably discharged from the US Air Force Reserve, I was honorably discharged from the NHL. And I was ready to retire.

The physical and mental fatigue that resulted from constantly wondering what was wrong with my knee, and whether or not it was fixable, was draining me. When I went up to Hartford, I had anticipated that Dr. Fulkerson would tell me what was wrong with my knee and how to fix it. When I didn't hear that, it was extremely disappointing, yet also a relief. I was somewhat vindicated for all those years of complaining about my knee, and sensing not a whole lot of support at times.

Forget playing NHL hockey. Even as a normal civilian, I was having issues. I was constantly wondering if I was going to trip and fall on the way to the rink. I held on to rails everywhere I went for fear of falling down the stairs. I was afraid that I wouldn't be able to get out of the way of an oncoming car while crossing the street in New York. I couldn't run three feet, yet I continued playing in the NHL.

Flyers owner Ed Snider was the first person to call me after my retirement fate was sealed. It was the very next day and my heart was sinking, wondering what was on his mind. I still had two years left on my contract. I was nervous about what Mr. Snider might say, and that this disappointing ending was going to get ugly from a financial standpoint. I felt bad enough as it was that I wouldn't be able to fulfill the contract for Mr. Snider and the Flyers.

The first thing Mr. Snider said was how disappointed he was. Not for him and the team, but for me. It was really amazing how kind and considerate Mr. Snider was in that emotional time. Although it didn't really surprise me. He said, "Jonesy, you played hard for me. You're a Flyer for life."

I was the luckiest guy in the world to have been traded to the Flyers when I was. I still had two years and over three million dollars left on my contract when I was forced to retire. It could have been a messy situation, but Mr. Snider turned it into a miracle. The Flyers paid me in full, and I continue to work with and for them to this day.

CHAPTER 20

"DUDE! YOU LOOK LIKE A BLOWFISH!"

Bob Clarke began my retirement news conference simply by saying, "Jonesy's done." A perfect ending to an unlikely career.

I remember thinking, "It is weird that this is happening." I had just turned thirty-two. But, I was also truly relieved after so many people had doubted how badly my knee was injured. Being an injured guy sucks. There is no other way to describe it. You go from a guy who loves playing hockey for the great game that it is, to a guy who is just trying to keep playing hockey as a business. As soon as you get injured, it goes from a game to a business. It's true.

I wasn't sentimental when I announced my retirement. I did, however, go back into survival mode. I had to find work in hockey. I knew that, despite what income I had made as a player, and what income I had coming, I still had to work. My knowledge of finances had come a long way since my signing bonus days. I needed a job and I wanted a job.

ESPN called and asked if I was interested in television work. They offered me a position as an analyst on NHL2Night, and in between periods of the games on ESPN2. I was always a good interview, and athletes like me who interview well after games usually get the first crack at TV jobs. A good interview doesn't always make a good television analyst, however, and I proved that right away. The first commercial break after my first few minutes as a professional analyst on ESPN2, I was covered in sweat. I looked like Albert Brooks in the movie *Broadcast News*. Responding to a question in the comfort of an NHL dressing room is a lot different, and a lot easier, than having something interesting to say on cue, under hot lights and wearing makeup. Plus, I gained liked thirty-five pounds within a few weeks of retiring. Keith Primeau left me a voicemail and said, "Dude! You look like a Blowfish!"

Besides being a lard ass, I made the mistake early in my television career of trying to be a TV guy instead of being myself. But I learned quickly, and by the end of my first year doing Comcast Sportsnet and ESPN, I felt like I could maybe make a living out of analyst work. And like everything else in my life, I made myself do it, as much as it hurt to do it. I painfully watched myself on camera, which as anybody knows, is awful and uncomfortable. I learned something constructive from it, and eventually got past the fear of being myself. And that's all the fear was. Everyone kept saying, "Be yourself, be yourself." Well, who the hell was I? That's what I had to find out.

As a kid growing up, being in the NHL was everything to me. Just like it is for millions of young, pre-adolescent hockey players around the world. As a teenager, the dream vanished as the reality of the likelihood of a hockey career began to settle in. Then, when I looked at those media guides while playing Junior C hockey, it all changed again. Out of the blue, out of nowhere, I said to myself, "I'm going to do this."

Twentieth century sociologist Robert K. Merton is credited with the expression "self-fulfilling prophecy." In his book, *Social Theory and Social Structure*, Merton gives the following definition: "The self-fulfilling prophecy is, in the beginning, a false definition of the situation evoking a new behavior which makes the original false conception come true."

And that is the perfect sentence to sum up what I chose to do when I was nineteen. I had a false conception when I thought I could make the NHL, considering where I was. But, I refused to accept that my dream wouldn't come true. I made myself believe that it would come true. I was going to go to college, I was going to get drafted into the NHL, and I was going to play professional hockey. And that was it. I didn't go out and train or work for it in a micro sense. It was always a macro-behavioral thing for me. I looked at the big picture and said, "I can do this." You can't begin to do anything in this life, against all odds, unless you tell yourself you can and picture it happening.

A lot of what I did, I did because I couldn't do anything else! I was a terrible student. I can't hammer a nail into a fence. I can't do anything. I have no skills. I don't know what I would have done without hockey. In practice, I couldn't figure out the drills. We'd do them everyday, and I still went to the back of the line to watch what the other guys did. I could never lead the drills. I'd see all these people flying around and I couldn't figure it out on my own.

As I look back on my hockey life, I might be more proud of what I do now as a broadcaster than what I did when I was a player. I studied Communications in college and quit because I was terrified of the camera. Hockey was easy for me compared to broadcasting.

What drives me today is the desire to continue earning for my family, to have a job and not rely on what I've put away, because who knows what's going to happen? The stock market could crash, a nuclear bomb could go off. Just keep working. Put your head down and skate. And that's how I practiced, too. I hated it. I hated practice. I have more fun preparing for a television show than anything I did as a player. But, I did love the games.

When I stop and think about what I'm doing now, and the city I'm doing it in, it's amazing. This is Philadelphia. A tough sports town. And for the most part, they've accepted me as one of them. And I am one of them. I'm just like anybody else. I just happen to talk about hockey, a game I used to play. I think I'm lucky to be like that, and I would never want to change. Working on the radio with morning-show-host-extraordinaire Angelo Cataldi at WIP has really helped me that way, because it gives people a chance to know who I really am on a daily basis.

OVERTIME

When I got called up to the Washington Capitals from the Baltimore Skipjacks in the fall of 1992, I didn't move to a new apartment or house. The Skipjacks and Capitals both practiced at the same facility, so I stayed in my condo despite the large increase in pay. Being a single guy who loved hockey, I would go to Skipjacks games at the Baltimore Arena if I happened to be home on an off night during the Capitals schedule. I wonder if any NHL players do that today? Do any of them go to AHL games in their free time?

One night I went to a Skipjacks game and met a guy named John Poor. John was a small and very thin young man with little bits of scraggly facial hair who always wore his Capitals jersey to the games. John and his dad had season tickets to both the Skipjacks and the Capitals. This was a big deal because the Poor family didn't have a lot of money. Not only did it take every extra penny to go to all of those hockey games, it took every effort as well. You see, John was in a wheelchair. He had cystic fibrosis.

Cystic fibrosis is a disease that affects the entire body, causing progressive disability and early death. Breathing difficulty, the most common symptom, results from lung infections. These infections cause inflammation, which clogs the airways and, over time, leads to lung disease. As the disease progresses, structural changes occur in the delicate organs and a number of problems arise. In the early stages, nonstop coughing, large phlegm production, and decreased ability to exercise are common. Many of these symptoms occur when bacteria that normally inhabit the thick mucus grow out of control and cause pneumonia. In the later stages of CF, changes in the lungs further exacerbate chronic difficulties in breathing. This is what John Poor faced, was facing and would face in the future. A future, in 1992, with little reason for hope, or even that much time.

One night, I struck up a conversation with John during a Skip-jacks game. Most of us don't like much about ourselves, but one thing I like about myself is that I've always had compassion for those less fortunate. It just comes naturally and I'm glad it does.

After a few games, we reached the point where we became such good friends that I would even go over to John's parents' house where he lived, and hang out with him and his family. It was a tiny house and they didn't have much at all. We would sit and talk hockey. John, despite his cruel disease, was always friendly and polite. John would talk hockey for hours and hours and he listened intently whenever I discussed any of the finer points of the game, including some of the funny stories behind the scenes. John listened to, or watched, every Capitals game. He knew all of the players, their bios, and statistics.

I admit, compassion was the force that caused me to go up to John Poor initially, but I stayed because of a genuine friendship. John was my age, he liked the same things I did, and he was fun to be around. Everything else about his life, health and economic status, were not really a factor at all. In the United States, hockey has a small but passionate following that creates bonds between strangers. If two people in their twenties both love hockey and meet somewhere, they will probably become friends. Especially at a game. The hockey rink has always been about bringing people together.

In 1955, children with cystic fibrosis were not expected to live even to the first grade. In 2005, the predicted median age of survival rose to thirty-six-and-a-half years, up from thirty-two in 2000. John was born around 1966, so at twenty-six, John was beating the odds for CF patients born in the 1960s.

John's parents would explain to me the status of John's health status and I would listen. His parents were older and they gave every ounce of their life to looking after him. They said the doctors told them that the air in the cold, dry rinks, as well as John's constant screaming and root, root, rooting for the home team, was actually good for his lungs. Hockey was extending his life.

But, like I said, I didn't care about John's condition beyond the fact that it was slowly killing him. I sat with John at games and hung out at his house because I enjoyed being around him. We were about the same age and we both loved hockey. His crappy disease and wheelchair status was something I didn't really think about in terms of our friendship. Yes, I obviously wanted to ease his pain with conversations and visits, but it wasn't a sacrifice at all to sit with him.

I would go to as many Skipjack games with John and his dad as my schedule would allow. Before the games, they'd come and pick me up in their rusty van. My Capitals teammate, Kevin Kaminski, started coming to some games with us as well. Kevin was a great guy who answered every piece of fan mail he received during his career with a handwritten letter of gratitude. If you think that's impressive, he also once amassed 455 penalty minutes playing for the Fort Wayne Komets in the IHL.

Anyway, Kevin got to know John as well. Slowly, John's health began to get worse and worse, and eventually he died. It was sad and strange to see this kid, roughly my age, deteriorate like that in front of my eyes. Kevin and I attended the funeral. We had a morning practice and then hit some traffic on the way to the funeral, so the Poor family delayed the proceedings until we got there. They wouldn't let the casket be closed until Kevin Kaminsky and I were able to view John one last time.

John Poor was buried in his Keith Jones Washington Capitals jersey. It was obviously a very painful and emotional time for me. But at the same time, what a gift it was to have known John Poor. It was a blessing to see all that John endured in order to experience a game and a culture that I already thought was great. There is no doubt, John Poor enriched my love of the game of hockey.

I can understand why some athletes do very little charity work. You get attached to people. They become family and when they die, it's tough. But, if you can do it, do it. It's worth it to them and to you. It helps keep your mind focused on the fact that when things are going good we are lucky. And when things are crappy, we're still incredibly lucky.

Like my brother's death, John's death was one of those things, where the pain that you feel gradually gives way to a new and deeper sense of perspective regarding your own life. It certainly reminded me of how lucky I was just to be alive, and doing something that I loved as well. I figured, if the alternative is not being here, why not make the best of every situation that you can without the fear of losing? Why be afraid of losing, failing, or trying, when the alternative is getting hit by a train of having your lungs ravaged by cystic fibrosis?

Why not take a chance and try to make something happen? Why care so much about what other people think of me? Why not fight to make an NHL team? Why not negotiate my own contract in shorts and a tee shirt? Why not steal Anson Carter's stick and play a shift with it?

Grieving the deaths of my brother and John Poor, and especially the manner in which they died, were, and continue to be, the two biggest influences on how I live my life. I had no fear of not making it. I had no fear of not being successful. Those tragedies relieved the pressure of looking at life as if I HAD to be a professional hockey player. I never felt like I had to, be because I knew there were so many people who had things a lot worse than I did. So, to me, hockey was never life or death. I had seen actual death up close. Twice.

That attitude also allowed me to be a fearless player. You would think not having a life-or-death attitude toward hockey would be a negative on the ice. If, in the end, it doesn't really matter, why put myself in danger? But, I did. So what if someone is coming to take my head off in the corner, or in front of the net, and I lose a few teeth.

How bad can it be considering what people like John Poor go through every day? That perspective helped me in every game I ever played.

But, the most important thing to me was that I never wanted to take a game off. As much as I joked and screwed around at practice, I really felt a sense of responsibility to that one fan who bought that one ticket for that one game that year. If I didn't play hard that one night, there might have been a John Poor in the stands whom I disappointed.

Despite being such cold places, hockey rinks are oddly warm and comfortable. They are playgrounds for kids and social clubs for adults. That put everyone on the same footing, even if that footing is on old, beaten down carpet in the rink "warm room." Incomes and social status don't matter in a hockey rink. John Poor was less fortunate than me in so many ways. He was on life's final shift with his health, and was, for all intents and purposes, poor. I, the same age, was a healthy professional hockey player making six figures.

But, the hockey rink, oblivious to economic status, brought us together and kept us together as friends until the day John died. I always had compassion for the less fortunate, and John only fortified that. But, John's compassion and kindness to the MORE fortunate, like me, was also a great example and lesson. Treat everyone with friendliness and a good manner no matter who they are and no matter what your lot in life is. It's really not that bad.

The cool, crisp, dry air in the hockey rink, the conditions that extend the life of ice, extended John Poor's life. To see this example of pure hockey love in my first full year of professional hockey was enough to last a lifetime. John knew he would die soon, yet he still lived life, went to hockey games, and rooted for the Baltimore Skipjacks and Washington Capitals. It gave his lungs and his heart comfort.

John's family was poor and he had very little in terms of worldly possessions. I'm sure there were thousands of people who walked past John at AHL and NHL games and wondered who he was. There was no doubt to me who John was every time he went to a hockey game.

It didn't matter if he came from a small house and drove a broken down van. I knew who John Poor was.

From meeting John Poor, visiting with John Poor, knowing John Poor, seeing John Poor in his casket with his Keith Jones Washington Capitals jersey on, and now looking back on John Poor's enthusiasm, friendliness, and decent, humble, good manners, I now realize who he truly was. Despite being blessed with so little in terms of health and money, John Poor was the richest man in the rink. The richest man in the rink.

John's love of hockey extended his life and enriched mine. He's the greatest role model I've ever had. A model for how to love a game, and how to live a life:

Put your head down and skate.

Acknowledgments

Co-Author John Buccigross would like to acknowledge and thank the following for making this book possible and somewhat plausible: Blake and Barry Koen of Middle Atlantic Press for giving Keith and I the means to construct this book and the complete artistic freedom to shape it. Every author/artist should get to operate like that. Keith Jones for his friendship, uniqueness and the opportunity to delve a little bit into his guts. Mom and Dad for the lifetime gift of words of music. Gail Last of the Niagara Falls Public Library. Hockey scout Sam Mc-Master. The Masterson brothers of Niagara Falls.

ESPN's Al Jaffe, Vince Doria, John Walsh, Judson Burch, Stu Mitchell, John Totten, Barry Sacks, Barry Melrose and Julie Mariash. The research department at ESPN which has every record, statistic, game, and nugget known to man or beast. TSN's Steve Dryden. 408 NHL goal scorer Ray Ferraro. 410 NHL goal scorer Ray Bourque. Dave Poulin. Jack Falla. Ray Onderisin.

Brett, Malorie, and Jackson for being renewable energy sources and letting Daddy write in peace. Melissa for making everything, and I mean everything, in my life possible and purposeful.

And for you the hockey fan. You are my kind of folk. First one's on me.